Exploring Political Worlds

Power, Dissent, Equality: Understanding Contemporary Politics

The complete list of books in this series is as follows:

What is Politics?
Jef Huysmans

Exploring Political Worlds
Edited by Paul Lewis

Politics and Power in the UK
Edited by Richard Heffernan and Grahame Thompson

Living Political Ideas
Edited by Geoff Andrews and Michael Saward

Making Policy, Shaping Lives
Edited by Raia Prokhovnik

The books form part of an Open University course DD203 *Power, Dissent, Equality: Understanding Contemporary Politics*. Details of this and other Open University courses can be obtained from the Course Information and Advice Centre, PO Box 724, The Open University, Milton Keynes MK7 6ZS, United Kingdom: tel. +44 (0)1908 653231, e-mail general-enquiries@open.ac.uk

Alternatively, you may visit the Open University website at http://www.open.ac.uk where you can learn more about the wide range of courses and packs offered at all levels by The Open University.

For availability of other course components visit the webshop at www.ouw.co.uk, or contact Open University Worldwide, Michael Young Building, Walton Hall, Milton Keynes MK7 6AA, United Kingdom for a brochure. tel. +44 (0)1908858785; fax +44 (0)19088 58787; e-mail ouwenq@open.ac.uk

Exploring Political Worlds

Edited by

Paul Lewis

The Open University

This publication forms part of the Open University course DD203 *Power, dissent, equality: understanding contemporary politics*. Details of this and other Open University courses can be obtained from the Student Registration and Enquiry Service, The Open University, PO Box 197, Milton Keynes MK7 6BJ, United Kingdom (tel. +44 (0)845 300 60 90; email general-enquiries@open.ac.uk).

Alternatively, you may visit the Open University website at www.open.ac.uk where you can learn more about the wide range of courses and packs offered at all levels by The Open University.

To purchase a selection of Open University course materials visit www.ouw.co.uk, or contact Open University Worldwide, Walton Hall, Milton Keynes MK7 6AA, United Kingdom for a brochure (tel. +44 (0)1908 858793; fax +44 (0)1908 858787; email ouw-customer-services@open.ac.uk).

The Open University
Walton Hall, Milton Keynes
MK7 6AA

First published 2005 by Edinburgh University Press, Ltd; written and produced by The Open University.

This edition published by The Open University.

Edited, designed and typeset by The Open University.

Printed in the United Kingdom by Bell & Bain Ltd, Glasgow.

The paper used in this publication is procured from forests independently certified to the level of Forest Stewardship Council (FSC) principles and criteria. Chain of custody certification allows the tracing of this paper back to specific forest-management units (see www.fsc.org).

ISBN 978 1 8487 3128 8

2.1

Mixed Sources
Product group from well-managed forests and other controlled sources
www.fsc.org Cert no. TT-COC-002769
© 1996 Forest Stewardship Council
FSC

Contents

Powers & structures

Centre & periphery

Participation & dissent

Equality & difference

Evidence & argument

The Open University course team

Geoff Andrews, *Staff Tutor in Government and Politics*

Brian Ashcroft, *Associate Lecturer Panel*

Pam Berry, *Compositor*

Karen Bridge, *Media Project Manager*

Vivienne Brown, *Professor of Intellectual History*

Julie Charlesworth, *Lecturer, Open University Business School*

Martin Chiverton, *Media Production Specialist*

Stephen Clift, *Editor*

Lene Connolly, *Print Buyer*

John Craig, *Associate Lecturer Panel*

Michael Dawson, *Course Manager*

Marilyn Denman, *Secretary*

Andrew Dobson, *Professor of Politics*

Lucy Flook, *Course Manager*

Fran Ford, *Course Secretary*

Liz Freeman, *Copublishing Advisor*

Robert Garson, *Reader in American Studies*

Pam Garthwaite, *Course Manager*

Carl Gibbard, *Graphic Designer*

Bram Gieben, *Staff Tutor in Government and Politics*

Janis Gilbert, *Graphic Artist*

Richard Golden, *Production and Presentation Administrator*

Montserrat Guibernau, *Reader in Politics*

Celia Hart, *Picture Researcher*

Richard Heffernan, *Lecturer in Government and Politics*

Wendy Humphreys, *Staff Tutor in Government and Politics*

Jef Huysmans, *Lecturer in Government and Politics*

Bob Kelly, *Staff Tutor in Government and Politics*

Paul Lewis, *Reader in Central and European Politics*

David Middleton, *Staff Tutor in Government and Politics*

Jeremy Mitchell, *Lecturer in Government and Politics*

Raia Prokhovnik, *Senior Lecturer in Government and Politics and Deputy Course Team Chair*

Michael Saward, *Professor in Politics and Course Team Chair*

David Shulman, *BBC Producer*

Lynne Slocombe, *Editor*

Mark J. Smith, *Senior Lecturer in Government and Politics*

Grahame Thompson, *Professor of Political Economy*

Consultant authors

Richard Freeman, *Senior Lecturer in Politics, University of Edinburgh*

Deborah Mabbett, *Lecturer in Politics, Brunel University*

Mads Qvortrup, *Professor of Sociology and Public Policy, The Robert Gordon University, Aberdeen*

Judith Squires, *Senior Lecturer in Politics, University of Bristol*

Nicholas Watson, *Professor of Disability Studies, University of Glasgow*

External assessor

Michael Moran, *Professor of Government, University of Manchester*

Preface

Tumultuous events such as '9-11' and the war and its aftermath in Iraq have reminded people how critical – and sometimes how deadly – the world of politics can be. Even the local, everyday politics of council services, schools and hospitals can affect people's lives powerfully. The Open University, with its unique tradition of interdisciplinary work and its mission to reach and enthuse a hugely diverse student audience, has set out to show why and how politics matters. It aims to shed light on the inner workings of power, decision making and protest, covering politics from parliament to the street, from ideas to institutions. *Exploring Political Worlds* examines comparative politics, asking what we can learn by looking at one country or context in the light of another. It sets out the tools we need to explore different worlds of politics, examining their strengths and limitations. Using a variety of case materials from a range of countries, it is a highly accessible entry point to comparative politics, distinctive for its clear and questioning reflection on the very methods used by students of comparative politics.

Series preface

This book is one of the five texts which make up the new *Power, Dissent, Equality: Understanding Contemporary Politics* series from The Open University. Each book in the series is designed for students and others who have not studied politics before, and can stand alone as a short introduction to key areas of debate within political science. However, if you wish to use the series as a whole, there are a number of references to chapters in other books in the series and these are easily identifiable because they are printed in bold type.

Each book offers a distinctive angle on the character and analysis of politics today. *What is Politics?* offers a critical overview, showing the often surprising faces and locations of political life. *Exploring Political Worlds* examines comparative politics, asking what we can learn by looking at one country or context in the light of another. *Politics and Power in the UK* questions how we might make sense of major developments and debates in UK politics, such as devolution and constitutional change. *Living Political Ideas* is an accessible introduction to key topics in political theory and ideology, such as legitimacy, national self-determination, dissent and social justice. *Making Policy, Shaping Lives* teases out and interrogates the many faces of public policy and policy making, drawing on case materials ranging from the single European currency to disability politics.

For all of the books, apart from *What is Politics?*, the chapters follow a common thematic structure. There are five organizing themes. *Powers and structures* explores the meaning and location of power in contemporary societies – what it is, and who has it. *Centre and periphery* looks at issues from the role of the state in our lives to the revival of nationalism in the post-Cold War world. *Participation and dissent* leads us to look, on the one hand, at voting and elections, and on the other hand at new and unconventional forms of political protest and dissent. *Equality and difference* examines how we are seen as 'equal to' and 'different from' each other and how this matters politically. The *evidence and argument* theme focuses attention on the ways in which the study of politics involves both explanation and recommendation.

Courses produced by The Open University are very much a team effort, and *Power, Dissent, Equality: Understanding Contemporary Politics* is no exception. Each member of the course team has made his or her mark on these books, and the work was done with goodwill and good humour. Some special thanks are owed. Raia Prokhovnik's tireless and dedicated contribution as Deputy and Acting Course Chair has been of huge benefit to the course. Mike Dawson has been a superbly calm, tactful and efficient Course Manager. Lucy Flook, Course Manager in the early days, played a significant role in getting the team up and running efficiently and ahead of schedule. Pam Garthwaite kept the momentum going in the period between Lucy's departure and Mike's arrival. The editorial skills of Stephen Clift and Lynne Slocombe and designs by Carl Gibbard have been key to the quality of the texts. Fran Ford has been a great support as course secretary, ably supported at different times by June Ayres and Marilyn Denman. John Craig and Brian Ashcroft have constituted a 'tutor panel' which has commented most helpfully on draft chapters. Robert Garson (Bobby) of Keele University was an influential and insightful member of the course team for two years. Professor Mick Moran of the University of Manchester has been the ideal external examiner – sharp and committed, he has been a tremendously positive influence on the content of these books.

Michael Saward, Course Team Chair

Introduction

Paul Lewis

This book is both a comparative introduction to politics and an introduction to comparative politics. In the two aspects, it is a concise introductory text and selective in its coverage of what we regard as key features of contemporary politics. As an introductory politics text, it sets out to explore some of the different worlds of contemporary politics and to help the reader develop a range of basic skills with which to understand them. In terms of comparative politics, it places the activity of national governments and culturally specific political behaviour in a broader comparative context that sheds new light on their role and meaning. Rather than attempting to provide a detailed map of the political universe, the book confirms the continuing importance of political inquiry and throws light on political matters that are shared by all humans – even if we are not always aware of them.

We focus on the existence of different political worlds because the nature and experience of political activity varies greatly across individuals, groups and separate countries. Any one of them can be seen as constituting a distinct 'political world'. Despite the huge emphasis now placed on issues and processes of globalization, and the impression this often gives of global uniformity, politics remains an area of enormous contrast and diversity. It might, indeed, be argued that the material foundations of contemporary social life and the very pace of technological change and innovation that provide the motor for globalization also promote political diversity and furnish the means for its expression. In any event, it is certainly not difficult to demonstrate that there are many worlds of politics and that a focus on the similarities and differences among them provide the very stuff of the comparative study of politics.

The idea underlying a comparative approach to politics is very simple – in the words of one classic account, 'to identify uniformities and differences and to explain them' (Macridis, 1955, p.1). We compare both to understand politics better, and to explain why political institutions and the activities associated with them take the form they do. It is something we do all the time – indeed, it is an activity we can hardly avoid. How do you respond to a question such as: what do you think of the present government? A standard response might be: in comparison to what? Should it be compared with the last one, or with the kind of government the opposition might have run if it had won the election, or with what we hoped or expected the government was going to achieve when it took office? The formulation of any answer thus often leads directly into the process of comparison. In this sense, an explicitly comparative introduction to politics is not very different from any other, apart from being characterized by a greater awareness that this is what we are doing and that comparison offers some advantages as well as imposing certain restrictions on how this kind of political analysis is conducted.

The main advantage is that a comparative focus makes the study of politics a more structured affair and promises to increase the rigour of its conclusions and, to that extent, make them more powerful. Some comparativists would go on to argue that the conscious use of comparative methods provides a form of control over otherwise 'wild' and intractable social processes that makes the study of politics a truly scientific one – although this is not a line of argument we need to pursue here in any detail. It will be examined further in Chapter 5 on the basis of the comparative analysis carried out in the different chapters of this book. A comparative focus also means that more attention is paid to the methods of inquiry that are used and the conscious strategy of comparison that is adopted.

Let us examine what this means: essentially, it means that employing a strategy of comparison involves making a number of choices (Roberts, 1978, p.288). First, it necessitates thinking about the appropriate unit of comparison. Different countries or states often provide the starting point for a particular comparative analysis. How does the UK, for example, differ from other countries in some important respect, say the quality of its democracy? More generally, the comparison may look at how states as a whole vary in the contemporary world and which particular forms they take (Chapter 2). But there are many different options and other avenues that could be explored. We might wish to compare the different regions of the UK – England, Northern Ireland, Scotland and Wales. Alternatively, we could consider the relative status of the people who live in the UK according to a wide range of criteria, such as occupation, age, sex, class, and nationality – or access to citizenship (**Huysmans, 2005**).

A second choice relates to the kind of comparison we are intending to conduct. Do we start by comparing units because they are very similar (the UK in the context of other democracies, for example) or on the basis of interesting differences (the UK as an established democracy compared with the new variants, for example, in post-communist Eastern Europe)? Further choices will then follow, and questions will arise about the choice of data (what are the measures of an effective democracy?), the context in which the unit is located (new or old members of the European Union, for example), and how far account is taken of other social dimensions (such as economic stability and processes of transformation).

However, comparison does not necessarily have to involve concrete political units, such as states or individuals. We might focus on how people perceive the political sphere and how the forms and substance of political activity can change across time and space, or how power can be understood and realized in different contexts. The possibilities are endless. The main point, though, is not which particular approach is taken or the actual techniques of inquiry employed on any one occasion, but how the nature and practice of politics can most effectively be understood and explained. Comparison is particularly useful in this context as it directs attention towards how similar (or different) political units relate to one another and why particular political outcomes are produced.

The five chapters in this book take up and explore these issues in a number of ways, and at the same time relate them to a number of themes in contemporary politics. In Chapter 1 the theme of powers and structures is explored. I first introduce the changing forms of contemporary political activity, and then examine the claim that it is changes in the values that people hold which is at least partly responsible for the apparent decline in conventional forms of political activity and growing mistrust of established political institutions. Comparative research shows a clear move in this direction in many countries of the world. Discussion of this topic is also linked with the different ways in which the dimensions of power and structures of political authority are perceived and constituted in the contemporary world. Important differences can be seen in the way in which people have understood the links between power and politics in different countries. These issues are then related to the others that arise, as we try to understand the character of modern democracy and make some assessment of its actual quality.

Chapter 2, written by Bram Gieben and me, directs attention to the state as the central political institution of the modern world and the primary structure through which power is exercised. As such, it has been the centre of many political networks, although this is a role that many would argue has been increasingly challenged by forces within the state's own periphery (local groups, subordinate nations, formerly marginal or excluded groups) and by the peripheralization of the state itself through processes of globalization and regional integration. The state, as the second section of the chapter puts it, is increasingly placed in question by a range of forces. But we see that in order to conduct an analysis of the contemporary state, we need to look carefully at what use of the term involves. The chapter then moves on to examine the process by which the modern state came into being and how it came to be such a dominant feature of modern politics. A comparative view of the different forms taken by the liberal-democratic state is then presented, and some conclusions drawn about the significance of the state in the contemporary world.

Chapter 3 is concerned with how and why people take part in politics. In this chapter, Mark Smith examines different forms of political participation in democratic systems and directs particular attention to the role of parties in channelling political activity and the reasons for their apparent decline. One of the reasons for changes in the pattern of participation is the transformation of political identity that has occurred in modern societies, although the institutional framework within which political activity takes place also has a major impact on political outcomes. The consequences of voting participation, for example, are significantly affected by the electoral mechanism in place, and the chapter examines the outcomes of the voting behaviour in different parts of the world. The chapter moves on to explore the differences between participation and dissent and the differences that can be detected between groups which work within the system and those which operate outside or against it. The declining interest in political parties is thus linked with an examination of social movements and the role of interest groups as alternative forms of political participation.

Judith Squires then takes up the theme of equality and difference. In Chapter 4, she analyses the theme in terms of plural identities and the different models of citizenship seen in contemporary European states. Citizenship rights are operative in a number of spheres – civil, political, social and cultural – each of which has become an area of lively political debate and places in question the way in which core values should be implemented in the contemporary political world. The different ways in which modern democratic states have tried to reconcile growing demands for equality with stronger pressures for the recognition of difference have produced four possible models of citizenship. In this context, actual citizenship practices are compared in different European contexts: Britain, France, the Nordic countries and Belgium. Each country (or group of countries) has broadly implemented one of the four different models, although most have been subject to recent change in response to the demands of minority ethnic groups and attempts to enhance the political inclusion of women.

Chapter 5 draws the book to a conclusion, and considers key questions about the interplay of evidence and argument in political analysis by directing attention to the alternative projects of story telling and theory building in comparative politics. In this chapter, Andrew Dobson begins by raising basic questions about what comparative political analysis involves and how the process has been conducted in the other chapters of the book. Particular attention is paid to questions of fact and value and to how the issue of cultural specificity can be addressed. Is it better, Dobson asks, to follow the comparativist in trying to build general theories about different societies which have wide applicability, or to tell (in the manner of the anthropologist) detailed stories about particular societies which carry a special meaning? Both, of course, have much to offer; but, arguably, it is only by developing and using the tools of the comparativist that we can hope to interpret political reality and explore the different worlds of politics in a scientific manner.

So, *Exploring Political Worlds* is a book that ranges widely over a variety of different countries, peoples and groups. It confronts a number of key issues in comparative politics, and at the same time provides an up-to-date account of major themes in the study of contemporary politics more generally. Major concepts, such as those of power, the state, participation and citizenship, are introduced and analysed in a broad comparative framework. Of course, both comparative politics and the larger discipline of political science to which it belongs have themselves changed and developed over the years. But the major concepts and key areas of discussion have not been greatly transformed. A recent publication in the field maintains that 'the sociopolitical world is constructed by human practice, and [our inquiry] seeks to explain how this construction takes place' (Green, 2002, p.15). That strikes me as an accurate description of what students of politics have been doing for some years – and a clear reflection of what we are aiming to achieve in this book.

REFERENCES

Green, D.M. (2002) 'Constructivist comparative politics: foundations and framework' in Green, D.M. (ed.) *Constructivism and Comparative Politics*, Armonk, NY, M.E. Sharpe.

Huysmans, J. (2005) ***What is Politics?***, **Edinburgh, Edinburgh University Press/The Open University.**

Macridis, R. (1955) *The Study of Comparative Government*, New York, Random House.

Roberts, G.K. (1978) 'The explanation of politics: comparison, strategy and theory' in Lewis, P., Potter, D. and Castles, F. (eds) *The Practice of Comparative Politics*, London, Longman.

Politics, powers and structures

Paul Lewis

Powers & structures

Contents

1   INTRODUCTION

In starting to explore political worlds we immediately confront the fundamental question of what political activity is actually about and the form that politics takes in contemporary social contexts. This takes us straight into another major discussion – that of the nature of power and how it is exercised. This chapter attempts to answer these critical questions.

2   CHANGING FORMS OF POLITICS

Politics, as a formal activity and established social practice, is in apparent retreat in many parts of the world. Only 59 per cent of the electorate turned out to vote in the 2001 British general election (a dramatic fall of 12 per cent from 1997); the membership of parties is at an all-time low (membership of the Conservative and Labour Parties each hovering around the 300,000 mark, having declined from over a million in 1982 in the case of the Conservatives, and even more – if the union bloc-vote is included – for Labour); sleaze and sharp practice are presented as the order of the day for many politicians; and Westminster sees more 'spin' than a dry summer's afternoon at Lord's Cricket Ground. Politics as a focus of interest and area of activity, in fact, often seems to be largely devoid of any real substance for much of the population.

This is not just a British phenomenon. In European democracies generally, electoral turnout has been declining steadily since the 1970s and party membership fell significantly in most of them during the 1990s. At 71.6 per cent, turnout during the first round of the French presidential election in 2002 was also the lowest seen during the Fifth Republic under the new voting system established by President de Gaulle. It contributed to the shock result whereby Socialist Prime Minister Lionel Jospin failed to get enough votes to go through to the second round and was beaten into third place by right-wing extremist Jean-Marie Le Pen.

Accompanying the growing popular disengagement from traditional politics there has also been greater instability, a rise in anti-parliamentary sentiments and strengthening of populist forces – trends that have not been restricted to established Western democracies. In the 2001 Polish election, only the fourth free election since the end of communist rule, neither of the two former ruling groups even received enough votes to gain any parliamentary representation at all. The 46 per cent of the electorate that turned out to vote sent representatives of four quite new parties to parliament, at least two of which expressed radical populist views fuelled by suspicion of European integration and doubts about the consequences of Poland becoming a member of the European Union.

Elections have increasingly become an occasion for the expression of general opposition to mainstream politicians and the rejection of established parliamentary processes. Growing numbers of voters ignore elections completely and simply do not vote (Figure 1.1). 'Anti-politics' has gained the upper hand in some quarters, and there is a growing tendency for people to turn their back on conventional political activity altogether. To some extent these views draw on well-established doubts about the nature of politics and the kind of activities in which politicians are involved. Uncomplimentary observations about politicians and the profession they follow have been standard fare for a long time, although perceptions do seem to have become even more negative in recent decades. Nevertheless, the level of turnout in the 2001 British election was not just a shock to observers and politicians in the UK: it also flew in the face of many recent findings and studies about the place of politics in modern societies.

FIGURE 1.1   Voting in the General Election, June 2001, St Mary's Church, Flowton, Suffolk. Voting is increasingly seen as a traditional and outmoded activity

2.1 Accounting for the decline in electoral turnout

The extent of the decline in turnout was puzzling for a group of British political scientists. It seemed to undermine leading accounts of the social factors underlying voting patterns. The accounts indicated that turnout would

FIGURE 1.2 Awareness of declining interest in elections is not new: a cartoon from the *Daily Mirror*, 12 October 1910

increase as education levels rose and people had higher incomes (Whiteley *et al.*, 2001; see also Figure 1.2). From other social scientific points of view, the 2001 developments were less puzzling but certainly did not carry the negative implications for political interest and orientations towards the political sphere outlined above. One approach drew on long-established international analysis of public attitudes. A major survey of global values, the World Values Survey, was carried out by Ronald Inglehart (1997) and his team (based at the University of Michigan, USA), who collected data from 43 countries across the world. They have charted people's changing attitudes and their social values since the 1970s, including people's views of different aspects of the political world.

Inglehart's findings provide a ready context in which to understand the low turnout in the 2001 British election and the political malaise in which it was located. He writes of a 'massive erosion of trust in government', signs of which were first noted in 1974; the erosion of institutional authority; and declining confidence in hierarchical institutions. People had less faith in the established organs of government and became less likely to support traditional political parties. The shift was a general one across many nations, but was characteristically sharp in the USA where, 'In one generation, the prevailing outlook had changed from overwhelming trust to overwhelming cynicism' (Inglehart, 1997, p.293).

However, this was far from being the whole story:

> Allegations of apathy are misleading: mass publics *are* deserting the old-line oligarchical political organizations that mobilized them in the modernization era – but, far from being apathetic, they are becoming more active than ever in a wide range of elite-changing forms of political participation.
>
> (Inglehart, 1997, p.307)

A comprehensive European survey produced very similar findings:

> West European citizens have not withdrawn into political apathy and disillusionment; on the contrary they participate more. What has changed, however, is the repertory of political action which has broadened since the 1960s and 1970s to include a range of direct or uninstitutionalized forms of action – petitions, demonstrations, citizen initiatives, political strikes.
>
> (Kaase *et al.*, 1997)

From another point of view, such developments reflected a perceptible narrowing of the range of political alternatives and the fact that increasing numbers of people see direct action as the only effective form of opposition to corporate capitalism. Anti-globalization movements thus gained extensive support in the late 1990s as a means of expressing opposition to the strengthening 'free-market' consensus. Enormous demonstrations against the Iraq war were organized in early 2003 and involved a wide range of people – including many schoolchildren. But such forms of activity also raise questions about what can be considered legitimate political activity and participation – or what politics itself means under contemporary conditions. For some people direct street action is best defined not as a form of politics but as riotous assembly, radical dissent or civil disorder.

Similar problems and questions of definition arise in less dramatic contexts, too. Noreena Herz (2002) in her widely read book *The Silent Takeover*, notes that:

> The politicians' star is fading. People recognise politicians' conflicting interests and unwillingness to champion them, and are beginning to abandon politics *en masse*. The British Women's Institute – the very symbol of comfortable Middle England – battled the Sainsbury supermarket chain over GM foods, but also slow-handclapped Blair.
>
> (Herz, 2002, p.11)

From another perspective, however, the change in attitude within the Women's Institute (Figure 1.3) was far from being an abandonment – it was more an unprecedented embrace of politics – and signalled the onset of a

FIGURE 1.3   A cool reception for Prime Minister Tony Blair at the Women's Institute Conference, Wembley Arena, June 2000

new activism. In similar vein, and capitalizing on the disillusionment with the major parties, single-issue groups and minor groups contested a record number of seats in the 2002 council elections in Britain.

2.2   Shifting values and the emergence of a new politics

At the very least these observations raise some fundamental issues and carry a number of implications. How far 'politics' extends beyond the formal institutions of government and state is a matter of considerable debate and much controversy (**Huysmans, 2005**). One implication, however, is particularly important for the topic of this book: there are in fact many different conceptions and indeed worlds of politics – both in a geographical sense (although World Values Survey findings hold true for most wealthy modern societies) and across time as a fundamental shift from what Inglehart calls materialist to post-materialist values is identified (Inglehart, 1997, p.312). Traditional 'materialist' values, emphasizing physical and economic security as the prime objective, have increasingly given way to 'post-materialist' priorities, more concerned with self-expression and the quality of life (see Table 1.1). People's concerns have been less dominated by basic issues of survival and directed more towards how a better and more satisfying way of life may be achieved. The shift has been particularly marked in southern Europe (Italy and Spain) and the USA (Table 1.1). 'Politics' therefore – at least in the developed world – does not mean the same thing in different contexts and at different times.

TABLE 1.1   The shift towards post-materialist values: results from 1981 and 1990 (post-materialist minus materialist scores)

	1981	1990	Net shift
Britain	−13	0	+13
France	−14	4	+18
Hungary	−50	−41	+9
Ireland	−20	−4	+16
Italy	−39	7	+46
Japan	−32	−19	+13
Spain	−41	−6	+35
USA	−24	6	+30
West Germany	−11	14	+25

Source: Inglehart, 1997, p.157

It was the context of social and political modernization (see Box 1.1) that promoted materialist values and saw many previously disenfranchised people being mobilized in political parties, trade unions and other formal and hierarchical organizations. This involved a process of political change in which many people gained the right to vote and were able to exercise more influence over government, giving them therefore greater confidence that governments were acting in their interests and enhancing trust in institutions of political authority. It is a period of change that has, however, now long ended in most modernized societies and people's values have changed, a transformation that has been accompanied by a strong disenchantment with the forms and institutions of what is now regarded as traditional politics.

BOX 1.1   **Defining features of modern societies**

1   Dominance of secular forms of political power and authority, and conceptions of sovereignty and legitimacy, characteristic of the large complex structures of the modern nation-state.

2   Monetarized exchange economy based on the large-scale production and consumption of commodities for the market, ownership of private property and systematic accumulation of capital.

3   Decline of the traditional social order, with fixed social hierarchies and overlapping allegiances, and appearance of a dynamic social and sexual division of labour.

4   Decline of a religious world view and the rise of a secular and materialist culture exhibiting individualistic, rationalist and instrumental impulses.

(adapted from Hall, 1992, p.6)

The large complex structures of the modern state are now perceived as delivering fewer benefits than they once did. From a related point of view, a 'new political culture' (Clark and Inglehart, 1998, p.9) has emerged to replace the traditional model of class politics. 'Anti-politics' can also, therefore, be conceived as a form of 'new politics' characteristic of postmodern society (although in the case of east European countries such as Poland it also seems to reflect patterns of political activity that can at least partly be seen as 'pre-modern'). We shall examine the implications of this shift in the next section, and focus more closely on what politics means in the contemporary world and the different contexts in which it is conducted.

SUMMARY

- There are distinct signs that conventional forms of political activity are in decline.

- But this can also be interpreted as a shift to a new kind of politics reflecting the adoption by increasing numbers of people of post-materialist values.

3 THE SUBSTANCE OF CONTEMPORARY POLITICS

The introduction of evidence on the spread of post-materialist values and the emergence of a new political culture opens a new perspective on the growing public disenchantment with conventional political activity. The substance of contemporary politics has in this sense become more diverse. It is a rather different world of politics that appeals to those with post-materialist values and has greater relevance in terms of the political aspirations and concerns of many contemporary citizens.

Post-materialist values have not been distributed equally among all members of modern societies. Broadly speaking, they have been more attractive to younger people and it was among those born in the years immediately following the Second World War that a distinctive increase in the proportion of those holding these values was first identified in western Europe. British studies suggest a slightly different divide and, predictably, it is from figures on patterns of television viewing and interest in political topics that some of the sharpest insights can be drawn. BBC analysis has thus shown that the 'under-45s are much more disengaged from politics, and it is not just boredom with party political coverage, but something more systemic. It poses questions about how this generation looks at politics' (*The Observer*, 3 February 2002). In short, there is recent British evidence to confirm the distinction drawn above between those still interested in traditional politics and others, perhaps more inclined to hold post-materialist values, who reject the conventional Westminster-focused activities or choose not to participate in such processes.

From another point of view there are yet further distinctions to be drawn: in addition to whether people show a high degree of political interest or not, research has shown that account should be taken of the degree of relevance that they attach to politics compared with other activities. Such investigations point to an interesting category of the contemporary citizen as a political spectator – those for whom politics may well carry considerable interest but does not necessarily seem to be very important. For such people politics has lost its obligatory character.

Both perspectives thus point to the importance of choice in this area, either between different kinds of political activity (in terms of traditional institutional politics or more direct action for those holding post-materialist values), or between those interested and participant in conventional politics and others more inclined to turn their backs on it. To this extent, politics has taken on the appearance of just one more consumer product that people can decide whether or not to buy into.

3.1   The political context of everyday life

In other respects the realm of the political has become more dominant, its reach that much longer and its effects more pervasive than ever before. There may well be elements of choice for the citizen, but political processes will continue to shape their lives whether or not they participate in or even take note of them. From this point of view, those who choose not to participate in politics or involve themselves in its processes or institutions are failing to exercise the political rights they do have and are handing over their powers – however limited on an individual basis – to someone else to use on their behalf. In contemporary societies political decisions and government authorities affect every aspect of our lives – from our waking moments (timed according to summer or standard mean time by parliamentary legislation) to the time we go to bed and turn out the light (no longer provided by nationalized industries in Britain but government regulated nonetheless). It hardly needs pointing out that the intervening work or education period is subject to diverse forms of control, regulation and support (and the subsequent income generally taxed at source), while leisure pursuits are equally limited by all manner of controls and restrictions with the general intention of securing public safety and serving the interests of the community as a whole.

Those who enjoy shopping or are simply obliged to satisfy their everyday needs on the 'free' market will also be aware that diverse forms of regulation operate here too, ranging from local council directives to the prescriptions of the World Trade Organization that our government representatives have agreed to support and implement. The apocryphal straight cucumber favoured by the agents of the EU is just one minor detail in this sea of government regulation and controls that emanate from political institutions, many of which we would be ill-advised to do without if we want to live in a reasonably secure environment. Regulations to ban the sale of poisonous foods, provide drinkable water, maintain the safety of motor cars and reduce levels of pollution are warmly welcomed, at least in principle, by most people.

Government regulations and parliamentary legislation are generally understood to be part of the political process, but they too are just one of its outcomes and by no means provide the only substance of politics or main focus of political activity. Politics, and even government, is not just about limitation and the regulation of human activity. Since the time of the ancient Greeks, politics has also been seen as part of the 'good life' (those who continue to see political activity as something rather sordid and largely distasteful might do well to read and ponder on Bernard Crick's comparison of politics with sexuality as related dimensions of the human condition: Crick, 2000, pp.25–6). The restrictive aspects of government and administration can be contrasted with more positive aspects of political activity. The limitation of detailed government surveillance and reductions in administrative control that became known as the 'rolling back of the state' can, indeed, also mean a strengthening of the political process, while decisions to reduce state powers or privatize government-controlled assets are themselves highly political acts, too.

3.2 Politics as a better life

One example of this strengthening of the political process is the changes that have taken place in former dictatorships and authoritarian countries in recent years. The closing decades of the twentieth century saw the end of communist dictatorship in many countries of eastern Europe and the introduction not just of some variant of liberal democracy but also of what Mouffe (1993) has called the 'return of the political'. This raises in a direct way the question of what politics is actually about. Politics, and the central activities with which it is concerned, may be defined in various ways and its basic character is the subject of much discussion and acrimonious debate.

Although most writers identify several key features, politics remains an essentially contested activity:

- Politics is, first (and least contentiously), a collective activity involving people who have some common identity or face shared problems. It is about defining what matters for a society (**Huysmans, 2005**).

- Second, the idea of politics assumes some kind of diversity or the holding of different views on how such problems should be tackled or solved; disagreement or conflict is acknowledged to be part of the political process.

- Third, it involves the reconciliation of such differences through discussion, persuasion or other essentially peaceful means of securing agreement, although it does not exclude the exercise of power and use of force to back up the implementation of collective decisions (Hague and Harrop, 2001, pp.3–4).

From this point of view, politics is one of the more satisfying and productive solutions to the basic problem of social order. It involves people confronting the existence of fundamental differences of opinion and sources of conflict while accepting that violence or repression is not the best way to deal with them. War, as Karl von Clausewitz wrote in the early nineteenth century, may indeed be 'nothing but a continuation of political intercourse with a mixture of other means' (Clausewitz, 2004, p.2) but for most people participation in a political process is an infinitely better option than the necessity of waging war.

The turn, or return, to the political as a solution to violent conflict and the underlying problem of social order can be seen on several continents and in a number of political contexts. One readily identifiable case in Africa was provided by Angola in early 2002 when the death of Jonas Savimbi, leader of the rebel UNITA (National Union for the Total Independence of Angola) forces, opened the way to the end of a 27-year civil war (aided and abetted for much of that period by the formerly competing superpowers of the Soviet Union and the USA). During that period a third of the country's population had lost their homes, half a million had been killed and twelve million mines had been laid, roughly one for each Angolan (Smith, 2002). Six weeks after Savimbi's death, UNITA signed an agreement with the government which committed their 50,000 soldiers to lay down their weapons and the government to hold 'free, just and transparent' elections. The process would be overseen by the USA, Russia and Portugal (as the former colonial power). The passage from military to political conflict was most directly expressed in UNITA's decision to transform itself at its next congress from a military organization into a political party. This embrace of the political did not, of course, mean that harmony would replace conflict but that political competition would – hopefully – succeed military warfare and put an end to the decades of violence. It was a change that at least promised to be less destructive of human life and limb.

Elsewhere, comparable changes had occurred some years earlier as the Soviet Union relinquished its hold over the satellite countries of eastern Europe and the Union itself then dissolved as the power of the Communist Party was broken. This 'return of the political' in the former dictatorships of communist eastern Europe brought major benefits to the citizens of those states in terms of the restoration of liberal democratic rights, free elections and a range of civil liberties. The end of some of the most extreme twentieth-century dictatorships has thus been followed by a resurgence of political activity and the opening up of largely closed societies to more spontaneous public activity and diverse civic initiatives. Dictatorships like those of the Communist Party and its various leaders in Soviet Russia (and its diverse allies in eastern Europe), as well as the analogous forms of rule introduced by Adolf Hitler in Germany and Benito Mussolini in Italy in the 1920s and 1930s, were indeed not just antithetic to democracy but in certain important senses destructive of the political sphere as a whole by virtue of their broadly 'totalitarian' character. Totalitarian rule has been regarded as fundamentally opposed to political activity and marks, in Crick's view, 'the sharpest contrast imaginable with *political* rule' (Crick, 2000, p.34).

Totalitarianism is, or was, based on ideological thinking which is 'an explicit and direct challenge to political thinking' in that it assumes and promulgates a set blueprint for social development which it is the task of government, largely self-appointed and under the control of a central leadership, to implement in the face of any opposition or alternative views (Crick, 2000, p.34). It eliminated all possibility of individual and group initiative not in line with the thinking of those who controlled the state and the single party that dominated it. The Marxist vision that underlay communist practice was thus premised on a vision of the 'end of politics', which was in turn optimistically based on a vision of the abolition of material scarcity. The restoration of the political sphere gave individuals and groups greater rights of self-expression and contestation in a broad social arena, the ability to pursue their interests in the public sphere and a greater capacity to work for their vision of the 'good life'.

3.3   A contrasting view of politics

Rather paradoxically, though, totalitarian societies were also often seen as being intensely politicized in that the totalitarian generally believes that everything is relevant to government as the whole society is mobilized for the achievement of the key principle that motivates the leadership – be it worldwide socialist revolution for the Soviet Union or the achievement of the German national ideal in the case of the Nazis. It is clear that a different conception of politics is involved here, and this highly negative view of politics was widespread among those who fought against communist rule. It was therefore a strong commitment to 'anti-politics' that motivated much of the east European anti-communist opposition in the 1980s and was best exemplified by the writings of the Hungarian George Konrád. Thus for Konrád (1984, p.92) 'Antipolitics is the ethos of civil society ... [it] strives to put politics in its place and make sure it stays there, never overstepping its proper office of defending and refining the rules of the game of civil society'. For Konrád, politicians were obsessed with power and had to be kept under strict control for the common good.

There are clearly radically different views of what actually is political – and even Crick seems to be in danger of combining them when arguing that totalitarianism is antithetic to political rule while observing that totalitarian societies themselves are intensely politicized. Part of the problem lies in the different conceptions of political activity that are in use, contrasts that underlie the contested nature of the idea of the 'political' in general. The three features of political activity identified above (in Section 3.2) refer to politics in terms of collective problem solving and the making of policy rather than its implementation. The implementation of policy is indeed primarily a function of the government process, although many people would see this as being set within a political framework as well.

The totalitarian cases demonstrate the different views very clearly. The citizens of such countries were almost totally deprived of power and had remarkably little capacity to influence decision making and form policy, and to this extent there was very little in the way of anything like a political process. Citizens had virtually no rights of opposition or public dissent, nor any capacity to contest political decisions or the means by which such decisions were arrived at. On the other hand, they were intensively governed by a powerful elite and mobilized within state institutions for the achievement of broader national goals – and in this sense public life was highly politicized. It might also be argued that there was a significant difference in such societies between formal politics, which was largely eliminated, and informal politics, which was indeed widespread but conducted secretly by those who had some access to power within government offices and the state administration.

People's view of politics is, understandably, strongly influenced by the place they occupy in the political system. As a professional writer with little personal political influence, George Konrád felt himself to be very much on the receiving end of government, a small part of a large political machine and a victim of power-hungry politicians. It was his response to this situation that fed his commitment to anti-politics and opposition to communist rule. Politics for Konrád, as for the great majority of people in the Soviet Union and its satellite countries, had very little to do with any collective problem solving (that was only possible within civil society) and was far more about the arbitrary exercise of power on a very large scale. The association of politics with the acquisition and exercise of power will be readily understandable to most people and is widespread today. It has provided one of the major strands in the analysis of politics since the late fifteenth century and the lifetime of the political philosopher Niccolò Machiavelli, and has invariably been the source of much criticism of politicians.

3.4 Politics and power

The focus on power and the activities of power-hungry politicians has tended to increase as the popular disillusionment with the practices of traditional politics, highlighted at the beginning of this chapter, has risen and an 'extraordinary decline' took place during the final years of the last century 'in the standard of public debate both among politicians and in the media' (Crick, 2000, p.281). But just as the world of politics cannot be reduced to the environment of the debating club and involves not only the identification of agreed solutions to common problems but also action being taken to apply those solutions – and thus the exercise of power – so politics also involves something more than just the process of acquiring power and a dominant concern with retaining it. Precisely how these components of politics can be fitted together and the different aspects combined to provide a general but broadly satisfying understanding of what political life is about is a complex and much discussed topic (see **Huysmans, 2005**). Some writers on the topic take a slightly different view from others, and some even disagree passionately with others.

There is, in fact, no single definition that adequately sums up the nature of politics as a whole, and the essence of politics can be regarded as something that is never fixed. The idea that politics is both about the ways in which the great affairs of state are settled, the dignified forms of parliamentary ceremony, and about the more sordid pursuit of individual interest and personal projection is its central paradox – and the point about paradoxes is that the conflicting propositions are indeed true. It should also be recognized that, as Galbraith (1986, p.216) has put it, in many cases the purpose of power is the exercise of power itself and that 'in all societies, from the most primitive to the ostensibly most civilized, the exercise of power is profoundly enjoyed'. All societies have 'rituals of obeisance' that celebrate the power holder and acknowledge the value of the institutions through which it is organized. But even if the issues concerning the abuse of power and the financial benefits that generally flow from power holding are set to one side, the status and esteem that accrue to those with power are less favourably viewed by those at the bottom of the political heap and provide a powerful source of resentment in a modern democratic society. Power is therefore both a prominent feature of any political world and a focus of political activity in its own right.

One of the best ways to understand the different aspects of political life is to investigate how power is exercised and political relations are expressed through political, economic and social structures organized in different contexts – in short, to explore the different worlds of politics, as suggested in the title of this book. This involves taking a comparative view and placing the experience of British politics, or that of any other single country, in a broader context.

S U M M A R Y

- A comparative perspective sheds light on the nature of contemporary British politics by drawing on a range of international findings such as those on the shift to different values and new modes of political activity.

- The diverse nature of political activity and its more positive features can be seen by comparing the British disenchantment with modern politics with the hopes attached to political rule following the civil war, Angola and in post-totalitarian societies.

- Distinctions made on a comparative basis between the role of politics and power through structures that can emerge in authoritarian and democratic societies show the different conceptions of politics that are currently in play and the different views of politics and power that can emerge when emphasis is placed on dimensions of collective problem solving or those of policy implementation.

4 WHAT IS POWER?

If power, the means of its acquisition and the nature of its exercise, provides much of the substance of politics we then need to examine what power itself is about and how it may be defined. It is easy to see that there is a basic ambiguity in the idea of politics – there is some disjuncture between the dignified management of affairs of state and the crude struggle for personal advantage that often seems to go on behind it. Many of these problems spill over into the analysis of power. Power, nevertheless, is often seen to be the very stuff of politics and its prime currency. In the political world it is power that makes things happen and turns the idea of government into something that works (more or less effectively) as a way of implementing collective decisions and steering societies in a particular direction. Just as money helps maintain the flow of goods and services in the economy, so power maintains the operation of the political system and helps get things done. Power even seems to be quite easy to comprehend at first glance – in our ordinary judgements and comparisons of political life we normally know what is meant perfectly well and have little difficulty in understanding one another. But pinning down the concept of power in precise terms is a more difficult exercise. Why not try it for yourself. How would you define power at the present moment? Which examples of power come immediately to mind?

4.1   The context of power

Obviously I cannot read your mind, but it is not difficult to identify some problems and further questions that crop up once the topic of power is raised. Is power some kind of 'thing' that can be identified, located and measured? If so, what does it look like, where is it situated and which units of measurement are actually involved? Reflection on all these possibilities soon leads to the conclusion that the concept of power is considerably more complex than it might at first appear. Examination of concrete examples of power is likely to raise a range of questions. In national (and British) terms the most likely place to locate power is in the office (i.e. the official role) of the prime minister. But some prime ministers seem to have been rather more powerful than others, so personal characteristics are also likely to play a part. How far, too, is the power of the prime minister constrained by structures such as relations with the cabinet, position in parliament, relations with the party whose parliamentary majority maintains the prime minister in office, or any other of a whole range of contingent circumstances that affect the exercise of power?

Power, though, is not purely a personal attribute, and relations with others in the government apparatus are involved. Which subordinates and political colleagues come into the picture here and are critical to the prime minister's capacity to exercise power? What are the institutional means by which prime ministerial decisions are actually implemented? All this, of course, ignores the broader context and the extent of the power that the British prime minister can exercise in relation to those of other countries and more powerful states. There is also the whole issue generally summed up in terms of 'globalization' and the shift of power away from the state, which suggests that today the power of any national leader is strictly qualified and limited by the broader economic, technological and political connections that now encompass the entire globe.

So we may indeed generally know what we mean when we make 'unreflective judgements' on power in society and are confidently able to state, for example, that the president of the USA has considerably more power than either ourselves or local town councillors. However, defining what power precisely consists of raises a number of serious problems. Power may well be a, or even *the*, key concept in the study of politics and many people may find it quite easy to accept this observation as a relatively uncontentious fact, but there are no immediately identifiable features or obvious signs of power itself. Some common statements help us to grasp different aspects of power, but they do not get us much closer to its essence. Power might well come out of the barrel of a gun – but guns and military hardware in general are not the same thing as power. Money in sufficient quantities can buy most things and empower people to achieve many of their objectives, yet material resources themselves are not quite the same thing as power. One common measure of power reflects the capacity of a community – and particularly that primary political organism, the state – to achieve its objectives. Thus the USA is not the largest country in the world and neither is it the most populous, but it is certainly the richest and most powerful (there is likely to be a close relationship between those two attributes, a factor which will certainly have to be taken into account).

Even the USA is not all-powerful: it has been shown to be vulnerable in a number of respects – as the attack on the Twin Towers on 11 September 2001 brought home to its citizens and the rest of the world with shocking immediacy. Its military might, despite being very large in relative terms, is also very limited, as shown in its enforced withdrawal from Vietnam in the 1970s. The outright physical power embodied in the technology and weapons under the direct command of military and government leaders should not, therefore, be identified with political power. Neither can sheer military capacity in terms of nuclear weaponry be translated directly into either military or political power, as both US and Soviet cases demonstrated quite graphically for much of the post-1945 period.

This is not a limitation that has suddenly emerged in the nuclear age. The mobilization of political, military and social resources by a totalitarian leader such as Hitler was no guarantee of success either. Nevertheless, it would be a mistake to think that because Hitler was not able to get what he wanted (lasting hegemony over central Europe) he did not have much power. The relation between power and outcomes is a complex and uncertain one. As Brian Barry (2000, p.186) has neatly put it: 'With enough power you can get everything you want without any luck. With enough luck you can get everything you want without any power. In between these two extremes, things get more complicated'. It is an observation not very different from that made some centuries earlier by Machiavelli, when he directed attention to the role of *fortuna* (or good luck) in political activity.

4.2 Deconstructing power

Power thus has many facets and is by no means easy to pin down. Any simple definition soon tends to be qualified by further observations or limiting conditions. If it is not a thing itself, what actually is it? Is it some kind of capacity, relationship or outcome? Many textbook discussions of power still begin with the classic account produced in 1938 by Bertrand Russell, the British philosopher, and later political activist in the unilateral nuclear disarmament movement (CND) of the 1950s and 1960s. His pithy observations are still useful as a starting point for a general discussion. It was not surprising, in view of the context in which his book on power was written, that Russell thought that 'War is the chief promoter of despotism, and the greatest obstacle to the establishment of a system in which irresponsible power is avoided as far as possible' (Russell, 1960, p.200). For Russell, power and its outcomes could be pinned down quite precisely, and power could be succinctly defined as 'the production of intended effects' (Russell, 1960, p.25). For example, despite the power held by Hitler and the threat he posed in 1938, in the long run it turned out that he was unable to achieve his aims and that the power he had at his disposal was not able to secure the intended effect.

Recent scholarly definitions have tended to be more abstract and rather more tentative than Russell's. One definition is that of power as 'the capacity to affect another's behaviour by some form of sanction' (Ball and Peters, 2000, p.34). This approach is located in a tradition influenced by the views of American political scientist Robert Dahl, who saw power in terms of the control of human behaviour. It is more concerned with power *over* people or opposing groups than with power *to* do something and the possession of a capacity to achieve particular objectives. Sanctions in this context may be positive or negative – involving either (or both) inducements or coercion, carrots and sticks. Power is also manifested in some kind of relationship – it is not just a capacity that inheres in one person in isolation from others. However, identifying cases where there has been a clear exercise of power can also be difficult and a number of other factors enter into the picture (Box 1.2).

BOX 1.2 | **Factors and problems involved in defining a power relationship**

1 Some kind of conflict is involved in the relationship between the two (or more) political actors concerned.
2 The consequences of the exercise of power have to be intended.
3 Any number of problems are involved in the 'measurement' of power (if it is indeed possible at all).
4 Elites or prominent individuals can often get their way without the overt exercise of power.
5 Questions of potential power also need to be taken into account.

Is it possible that these and other rather different insights can be fitted together to produce a single but generally satisfying definition? Power may well, as Russell suggested, be the fundamental concept in social science, but it is that very importance that makes it difficult to define the concept adequately. The many analysts of society are interested in many different things, and what people will regard as an adequate definition will depend on precisely what is of interest to them. Nevertheless, we need some kind of working definition to help us on our way. Lukes's suggestion, which he calls a 'very thin one', is to start from the basic observation that 'to have power is to be able to make a difference to the world' (Lukes, 1986, p.4). On this basis an interest in power is likely to direct attention to two areas of investigation and two further kinds of question:

- What is the difference that is made to the world?
- What is the nature of the process by which the difference is made?

4.3 Dimensions of power

It seems clear that any discussion of 'power' as a single category is too general and insufficiently focused to allow us to develop further any empirical analysis of political life. One of the major points here is that concern with the intentions of power holders is often too simple to do justice to the realities of actual power situations, and that consideration of the power holder's interests is often more important than personal intentions. A simple example of power in this sense might be ownership of a substantial area of land which ramblers and casual walkers may be unable to pass over because there is no public right of way. Such an outcome may be totally unintended (at least in an individual sense), but it is a direct outcome of the property owner's interest in the unrestricted right to enjoy and dispose of his or her own property. Lukes (1986, p.9) draws our attention to one of the key questions to be asked about power from this point of view: who can adversely affect the interests of whom? This is a view that leads to a discussion not so much of different definitions of power but of what has been called the different dimensions of power.

The *first dimension* is that exemplified in classic political science texts on decision making and American community power studies such as that pioneered by Dahl (1961). It is a view of power that focuses on the behaviour involved in the making of decisions on issues in which a conflict of interests can be observed and where power struggles are expressed as distinct policy preferences favoured by those involved in the political process. The exercise of power in this case is equated with the capacity to prevail over the contrary preferences of other people. Power is not envisaged as being exercised from a single political centre and different political tendencies often conflict and, in power terms, cancel one another out. Nevertheless, some preferences and policies will clearly prevail over others.

The broad conclusion drawn was that power in the medium-sized US communities during the early period after the Second World War – and, by extension, in the USA more generally – was distributed among different groups relatively equitably, that the US political system was pluralist in structure in this sense and that there was no clearly dominant class or power elite, as others had argued (Figure 1.4). This outcome was very much in line with the optimistic and rather self-congratulatory view taken of US democracy in mainstream political science and public discussion more generally during this period.

FIGURE 1.4 A US town hall meeting, April 1947, New Hampshire

The flavour of this account of US politics and its analysis of what power was like in the town of New Haven, USA, in the 1950s can be seen in a short extract from Dahl's book. It focuses on the issue of urban redevelopment, a policy that was pursued in New Haven with particular vigour and success by Mayor Richard C. Lee:

> What Lee did as mayor was to push redevelopment and renewal to the centre of focus and hold it there year after year. He determined that a large share of energy, time, skills and money would go into redevelopment. He devoted most of his own time and attention to it. He saw the need for a Citizens Action Commission and an extensive system of subcommittees, knew what kind of men he wanted for the CAC, persuaded them to accept membership, brought in Logue [the development administrator], induced him to abandon his attempt to start a law

practice in order to work full-time on redevelopment, identified himself fully with redevelopment, and made it into a major issue of his unceasing campaign for re-election ... he had managed to identify himself with a program of enormous political potentiality that in time might make him a serious contender for higher office ... If the Mayor and his redevelopment team were more successful than any other individuals in initiating proposals for redevelopment and renewal that were later adopted, their success rested on their capacity for anticipating what the organized interests, the political stratum, and the voters in general would tolerate or support.

(Dahl, 1961, pp.126–7, 140)

The 'difference made to the world' (Lukes's 'thin' definition of power), in this case of urban redevelopment, was therefore largely attributable to the astute judgement and vigorous activity of the mayor as elected leader, and to the conviction that success in this area would further help his political ambitions. His careful management of the local government structure and capacity to satisfy local interests were also essential factors in the successful exercise of power. Critics of this line of research, however, were quick to link its conclusions with the methods used by the investigators and the conception of political power that underpinned their work, linking this with an alternative view of power.

The *two-dimensional view* of power that was then developed involved consideration of what has been called the 'mobilization of bias', a political situation in which power is exercised by controlling the agenda and where only some issues are defined as important and thus subject to public decision. This has been most strikingly charted by other American political scientists, Bachrach and Baratz. Dominant groups – i.e. power holders – can decide which issues are important and politically relevant, and thus open to public discussion and eventual decision. Issues that are likely to be contested in ways that threaten the interests of the powerful can be removed from the public agenda, and do not become the subject of formal decision-making processes or the object of public conflict at all. An early view of such a situation was presented in the following way:

Of course power is exercised when A participates in the making of decisions that affect B. But power is also exercised when A devotes his energies to creating or reinforcing social and political values and institutional practices that limit the scope of the political process to public consideration of only those issues which are comparatively innocuous to A. To the extent that A succeeds in doing this, B is prevented, for all practical purposes, from bringing to the fore any issues that would in their resolution be seriously detrimental to A's set of preferences.

(Bachrach and Baratz, 1962, p.948)

This is a dimension of power that has considerable contemporary relevance and bears on the conduct of political life in many established democracies. As distinct from the period immediately after the Second World War, for example, the question of whether major industries should be nationalized just does not appear on any serious political agenda, even in the case of the British rail system where the weaknesses of economic privatization have become glaringly apparent. A focus on the control of the public agenda of political discussion and decision making can to some extent also be linked with the practices of the political spin-doctors whose activities now attract so much attention and popular criticism. Much of current political activity is, indeed, concerned less with the discussion of matters of public importance and decision making on issues of common concern than with matters of political presentation and the manipulation of agendas to keep sensitive or inconvenient matters away from public gaze.

Finally, a *three-dimensional view* incorporates all the insights into the nature of power offered by the first two dimensions but further emphasizes the role of political interests and encompasses the view that people's desires and beliefs may be modified and shaped in ways that can be seen as opposed to their underlying interests (Lukes, 1974, p.24). It is not difficult to link this perspective with the manipulative tendencies in modern politics that go beyond control of the public agenda to shape people's political preferences and involve forms of influence that can be broadly classified as thought-control. Politics can become, as suggested earlier, just one more consumer product for which demand can be created by an all-embracing public relations industry. While introducing a further refinement in the study of power relations, it also raises complex questions about the role of conflicting interests and how these interests may be defined, particularly if people are not personally aware of them.

All three dimensions nevertheless present treatment of the agenda as a key political issue: how to get issues on to it, how to keep them off the agenda, and how to make the political agenda just look like common sense. Different political structures are being used in each case. Such struggles have in common the assumption of a hierarchical model of power, one largely controlled by elites but subject to greater or lesser influence from other groups such as pressure groups, social movements or other segments of the population.

Lukes's discussion of the three dimensions of power presents three distinct perspectives that also move the focus of attention from the role of *agents* in the accumulation and exercise of power (elected leaders and the representatives of political groups, for example) to the *structure* of interests that shape power relations by modifying people's desires and beliefs. The ideas of French philosopher and social theorist Michel Foucault (1926–1984) took this line of argument forward, and he developed a radically alternative vision of power that departed yet further from the traditional assumptions of sovereignty and individual autonomy that have continued to underlie much contemporary analysis.

His vision went beyond the idea of society being structured or ruled by any kind of political agenda; it saw power, not as a distinct entity residing in a particular place or institution, but as a quality dispersed throughout society in different locations and a myriad of separate political sites. In this, Foucault effectively outlines a *fourth dimension* of power in present-day political life. He was quite emphatic in his view that 'power is not an institution, and not a structure; neither is it a certain strength we are endowed with; it is the name that one attributes to a complex strategical situation in a particular society … Power is everywhere; not because it embraces everything, but because it comes from everywhere' (Foucault, 1981, p.93). He also argued that power was a property inherent in a whole range of, if not all, social relations and had to be analysed as something that circulated throughout them, and only functioned in the form of a chain. Power is not, then, a distinct entity residing in a particular place or institution but a quality enmeshed in a network of social relations.

This is clearly a very different conception of power and its relation to identifiable social and political structures, an interpretation that reflects an awareness both of the pervasiveness and uncertainty about power relations and where they are actually located in contemporary society. It is not a view that directs attention to the formal political agendas, which in various ways constitute the prime focus of the three dimensions identified in Lukes's account, but one which takes account of the pervasive and diverse sites of conflict and contestation that characterize contemporary society. There is a broad movement away from institutionalized and hierarchical conceptions of politics that directs attention towards diverse social struggles and contests and is more issue driven. It is an approach that combines insights from philosophy, history and psychology (the quotations that appear above are taken from Foucault's *History of Sexuality*, for example), and by virtue of its originality and far-reaching nature Foucault's work is highly illuminating. He recognizes the power implicit in social practices generally seen as outside the realm of politics – such as those associated with sexuality, the control over people's lives exerted by apparently objective regimes or bodies of knowledge such as those represented and practised by the medical profession or criminologists, or even the way in which people's lives are shaped by specific forms of architecture (such as that of prison design). Power thus becomes internalized, and is exercised more by self-censorship and the shaping of individual desires than by external agents or visible structures of power.

This view of power is still not disconnected from the major institutions of political rule. Foucault directs attention, for example, to the major change that took place from the seventeenth century in the nature of the state as it increasingly came to be seen as an end in itself. This is associated with the idea of 'biopower' in the form of technologies used for 'analysing, controlling, regulating and defining the human body and its behaviour'; its people were increasingly thought of as resources 'to be used and taken care of to ensure the development and viability of the state' (Danaher *et al.*, 2000, p.64). Processes of control, regulation and surveillance are further intensified by the rapid spread of new technologies. In this sense the eye of the state may be seen today on many street corners in the form of CCTV cameras; British streets currently host ten per cent of the world's total of these machines, although the population is largely oblivious to this form of observation. Considerably more public resistance is aroused by the growing number of speed-cameras on the roads, presumably because they have a greater capacity to affect people's behaviour whether or not drivers infringe the speed limit. The exercise of state power through the location of roadside cameras has proved to be remarkably effective, regardless of whether they are actually operational. Power is therefore diffused throughout society and appears in some unlikely places – including little yellow boxes installed on the side of our roads.

Uncertainty about the nature of power, in both general and specific terms, and whether it can be located in or around any particular structure is, therefore, evident in many areas of political analysis. Debate continues about where power comes from and how it is exercised, and how power relations may best be conceptualized. While positive solutions to the questions arising from these issues may be difficult to identify, it is at least becoming increasingly clear that power is not so closely or unambiguously associated only with political leadership, the state, its personnel, institutions and processes, as it used to be.

SUMMARY

- Power is central both to the practice of politics and to its analysis as an object of study.

- It is remarkably difficult to define and attempts to pin it down involve elements of capacity, control and outcome.

- It is linked with elements of military capacity and material wealth, but is not identical with either.

- At the very simplest, power is about people being able to make some kind of difference and being able to make an impact on the world.

- Contemporary political studies have distinguished between different dimensions of power which focus on decision making, the determination of political agendas, the capacity of people to pursue their interests and Foucault's view of power as a chain of influence.

- Foucault's conception of diffuse, societal power reinforces the idea of an anti-hierarchical contemporary politics shaped by post-material values and split into a range of specific conflicts and localized issue-driven struggles.

5 WHERE IS POWER?

The focus on the different dimensions of power and the links between them show some of the complexities that underlie the problems of definition in this area and why the nature of concrete power relations can be so difficult to pin down. One of the major problems involved in identifying power holders – on the assumption that our conception of power suggests that such individuals exist – is that power is often a background attribute of a more diffuse political relationship, and that the mechanisms of power cannot be observed as it is in the process of being exercised. The sanctions associated with power and which ensure people's obedience to its dictates – that is, the force (whether physical, economic, intellectual or emotive) that underlies power and secures the implementation of a decision – do not generally need to be applied in many routine political situations.

We frequently accept that some people are power holders and that they have the means to back up their commands, decisions or even suggestions without requiring the proof that they do actually have these political resources. Power that is accepted in such situations, where the capacity for enforcing decisions remains implicit, is generally termed *authority*. Political authority is often understood to involve the exercise of power in ways that are legitimate, and for this reason acceptable to those involved in the power relationship. A boss may propose that an employee should perform an additional task, involving overtime, a special trip or unusual physical exertion, on the understanding that this is part of the job and that unemployment or clear economic disadvantages will follow if the 'suggestion' is not acted on. Children certainly used to be 'asked' to clear up their mess on the understanding that a smack or some form of punishment would follow if they did not do as they were told.

It is in connection with the state and the central institutions of government that the issues of power and authority emerge most clearly. Power is exercised not just by individuals but also, and even primarily, through particular structures such as government agencies and the diverse institutions of state. Many people we meet in the course of conducting everyday business and whose decisions we generally have little choice but to abide by – ranging from traffic wardens and police officers to tax officials and health inspectors – exercise power not on the basis of any personal qualities but because they occupy a formal office (in the sense of having an official status) in some government institution, public agency or structure of power.

The authority they have derives from the superior powers they represent and, in the final analysis, on the sanctions they can bring to bear on us to do what we are told. After warning letters, bailiffs and law-enforcement officers, this process plugs into the legal system and involves use of the capacity of those who govern us to fine us or put us in prison. Not so long ago, the legal system and the state that lies behind it in the UK could also take our lives if our misdemeanours were that serious. They still can in many states of the USA. When substantial numbers of people are involved, or the crisis is particularly severe or widespread, the border between criminal activity and armed insurrection is crossed and military forces become involved in imposing order and maintaining both the power of the state and the authority of its governors.

5.1   The central role of the state

From this perspective, power in modern societies, and the political processes that reflect and embody that power, are thus largely embedded in structures and institutions rather than being the affair of particular individuals. The emphasis on formal institutions would be contested by Foucault and others holding different views of the nature of power. It is, nevertheless, on the basis of this insight that we return to the widely held view that political activity is largely concerned with government institutions and processes and with activities embedded in the state. It is, indeed, the state that occupies the central position in modern politics and contemporary political activities because it is the primary locus of political power – and has essentially been so in Europe since the fragmented authority structures of medieval kingdoms and other forms of political unit were superseded in the early modern period (the nature of the state will be discussed in greater detail in Chapter 2).

In terms of the widely discussed disillusionment with contemporary politics and the structures of the modern state referred to earlier – relating to the lack of trust and confidence in those who make their living from it and the increasing distance many people feel from the established institutions of government – it is also the problematic nature of contemporary political *authority* and the role of the state that is primarily at issue. It is (as noted in association with the findings of Inglehart discussed earlier in this chapter) the erosion of *institutional authority* that underlies the prevalent malaise in many established democracies rather than the surfacing of a crisis of power or legitimacy. State action is increasingly seen in negative terms as unjustified intervention and the power of the state as less legitimate, making the state less authoritative as an institution overall.

The power resources of long-established states in the developed world are generally quite sufficient to ensure their continued existence. Few people would argue that the democratic order is actually not legitimate in general terms, although a prolonged crisis of authority would probably help produce this outcome, and it would also eventually come to bear on state power and the nature of the political resources that the state leadership was able to command. However, despite the extensive debate and controversy about the quality and effectiveness of the political process in the UK and other established democracies, it is not in these countries that state power has been seriously threatened.

State power has in fact been far more fragile in Africa (Somalia, Liberia, Sierra Leone) and in some countries of Latin America (such as Argentina, where a combination of incompetent and corrupt government and progressive economic collapse threatened the foundations of the state as a whole in 2001). A number of countries in Africa are now recognized to be what people often term 'failed' states, although the precise criteria by which we should judge failure or success in this respect have not been spelt out. Generally, however, unitary states (which are governed in most significant respects from a political centre) in most of the developed world have the capacity to survive and reproduce themselves. This does not mean of course that particular governments cannot be swept away or (more rarely) the specific political regime or constitutional order transformed. It is also less true of federal states, whose component units have considerably more autonomy and often have a right of secession. More frequently it is the political authority of the state's leaders and institutions that is challenged, and this produces a range of different outcomes.

The sudden collapse of the communist regimes in eastern Europe between 1989 and 1991 and the transformation of the states that began with these changes – events that both changed the political character of modern Europe and shifted the balance of global power – shed further light on the relation between the different dimensions of power, authority and legitimacy. The Soviet Union, for example, was never such a strong state as some people thought on the basis, for one thing, of a simple headcount of its nuclear missiles and the number of military personnel its leaders were able to command (Buzan, 1991, p.98). Its political resources and capacity for effective rule were in many ways strikingly limited and were stretched yet further by the insistence of the Soviet leadership, at least until the final phase of Mikhail Gorbachev's tenure in the top job, to retain detailed control over much of the national economy. When Gorbachev started to reform the Communist Party and reduced its power to intervene in many areas of the economy and political system, both the authority and power of the state began to crumble with striking rapidity.

5.2 Power beyond the state

The attempt to situate power in contemporary politics is a complex and intellectually (and politically) challenging process. Once the state-centred perspective is qualified the investigation can lead in one direction, for example, to the re-examination of the human psyche conducted by Foucault, and in another to the global economy and ideas about the 'internationalization of the state'. Many people now believe that the main centres of power reside beyond the state in a small number of international corporations and financial institutions with strong links to major decision makers in the USA. There has been, in Noreena Herz's words, a 'silent takeover' of the world of politics by the great transnational corporations, one of whose major consequences has been the death of democracy (Herz, 2002). Others see the transformation and ongoing process of change as one of considerably greater complexity. The huge transnational corporations may indeed have tended 'to make nation-states merely instruments to record the flow of commodities, monies, and the populations that they set in motion', but the contemporary phase of capitalist development is by no means 'adequately characterized by the victory of capitalist corporations over the state' (Hardt and Negri, 2001, pp.31, 307). One recent conception of 'empire' as a developing form of global interaction and rule roots it firmly therefore, amongst other things, in specifically American but also *political* interpretations of constitutionality.

Precise definition of the power cluster that has emerged in this context is by no means easy. One useful description is based on the French word used in this sense and elaborated by Robert Cox (1997, p.60) in terms of a *nébuleuse*, 'a loose elite network of influentials and agencies, sharing a common set of ideas, that collectively perform the governance function'. There is, in this conception, no formal decision-making process and no clear centre of power; instead there is a group of unofficial conclaves (the Trilateral Commission, Bilderberg conferences, world economic meetings held in Davos) and diverse inter-governmental bodies (the Organization for Economic Cooperation and Development, meetings of central banks, the International Monetary Fund, World Bank and World Trade Organization). (See Figures 1.5 and 1.6.) In such a form, Cox (1997, p.61) argues, the '*nébuleuse* is capable of shaping state policy and is very largely unobstructed by democratic control or accountability'. To the extent that global power is also partly state-centred the state that looms largest is – hardly surprisingly – the USA, and the context in which political power is exercised is one strongly conditioned by economic processes.

The major forces driving this process can be traced back to the 1970s and responses to the end of the post-war boom, the resurgence of neo-liberalism overseen by President Reagan and Prime Minister Thatcher and the renewal of Cold War politics that ultimately led to the defeat of Soviet Communism. Underlying this realignment were the problems that surfaced in the global economy, the emergence of new technologies and reorganization of labour and productive forces, but also more explicitly political perceptions that the established democracies were becoming increasingly unstable and potentially ungovernable. The influential Trilateral Commission drew the bald conclusion that Western states were suffering from an 'excess of democracy' and argued that state overload could only be tackled by the demobilization of the groups which were continually making new and ever more costly demands on the established authorities (Cox, 1992, p.33).

This has been seen as a 'great transformation' in the structure of modern capitalism, analogous to the fundamental changes that took place around the middle of the twentieth century which saw the stronger regulation of market

FIGURE 1.5 G7 finance ministers at work during the 1996 economic summit at Lyon, France

FIGURE 1.6 The public face of the IMF (amidst logos of other international organizations), Washington, 2002

economies and the establishment of welfare states in many countries. The recent transformation has been responsible for the strengthening of economic power relative to that of the strictly political. It has placed greater emphasis on the role of what are called free-market processes, although some large units (such as the huge transnational corporations) are much freer than the great majority of individuals, other organizations and even many states to influence the way these processes operate. One major consequence was a marked rise in indices of socio-economic inequality in the USA and other developed Western countries that followed this path of development. The share of marketable net worth held by the top one per cent of Americans had, thus, fallen by 10 percentage points between 1945 and 1976 but rose by 39 per cent up to 1989 (Blyth, 2002, p.272). This trend continued during the period of leadership by such 'centrists' as President Clinton (1993–2001) and Prime Minister Blair (1997–), but seems to have been intensified under the Republican administration of President George W. Bush (2001–), who in 2002 and 2003 proposed wider-ranging tax cuts and the abolition of inheritance tax.

Changes in patterns of politics and global governance have thus had significant social consequences. They represent a major transformation in the structures of power at both national and global levels, as well as reflecting important changes in the nature of both political and economic institutions, the means by which they operate and ways in which they relate to one another. Like power itself, the structures in which power is embedded and through which it is exercised are the object of extensive debate and much political controversy. The institutions of power, it may be argued, would seem to leave little place for the individual (or the agent of a particular action) or for the role of ideas. But this view is not universally shared. According to Blyth (2002, p.275), 'It is only by reference to the ways that agents think about their condition within an uncertain evolutionary order that the path of institutional change can be fully explained'. The nature and effects of power may indeed be conditioned by the structures in which it is embodied and through which it is exercised – but they are by no means determined or fully defined by them.

SUMMARY

- The broader discussion of power takes account of authority and the structures within which both power and authority operate.

- The state is central to the way power and authority are often understood and is a primary structure for the accumulation and exercise of power in contemporary societies.

- Some views challenge assumptions about the prominence of the state in relation to contemporary structures of global power.

- Contemporary power relations seem increasingly difficult to pin down in terms of political institutions and are critically enmeshed with economic processes. Like the idea and practice of politics itself, the nature of power and the structures through which it is exercised remain contested and the subject of extensive change and controversy.

6 CONCLUSION

The discussion carried out in this chapter now brings us back to the observations with which it began. It has directed attention to the following key features of contemporary politics.

- There is popular suspicion of orthodox politics and participation in established political institutions is declining – accompanied by the spread of new political values and more direct personalized forms of activity.

- The growing diversity of contemporary politics confirms the traditionally ambiguous nature of political activity and the contrasting views taken of it.

- The political world is intimately connected with questions of power, together with further debate and questions about the conceptualization of political life.

- Structures of power and authority are prominent in people's everyday experience and the shaping of their political life.

- There is continuing debate about where the centres of power are located, how it is exercised and whose interests are best served by it.

REFERENCES

Bachrach, P. and Baratz, M. (1962) 'Two faces of power', *American Political Science Review*, vol.56, pp.947–52.

Ball, A.R. and Peters, B.G. (2000) *Modern Politics and Government*, London, Macmillan.

Barry, B. (2000) 'Is it better to be powerful or lucky?', *Political Studies*, Special Issue, pp.186–95.

Blyth, M. (2002) *Great Transformations: Economic Ideas and Institutional Change in the Twentieth Century*, Cambridge, Cambridge University Press.

Buzan, B. (1991) *People, States and Fear* (2nd edn), New York, Harvester Wheatsheaf.

Clark, T.N. and Inglehart, R. (1998) 'The new political culture: changing dynamics of support for the welfare state and other policies in postindustrial societies' in Clark, T.N. and Hoffmann-Martinot, V. (eds) *The New Political Culture*, Boulder, Colorado, Westview Press.

Clausewitz, K. von (2004) *On War*, Chapter VIII, Section B, trans. Graham, J.J. (first published 1873), http://www.clausewitz.com/CWZHOME/On_War/Bk8ch06.html (accessed 27 February 04).

Cox, R. (1992) 'Global perestroika' in Miliband, R. and Panitch, L. (eds) *New World Order? Socialist Register*, London, Merlin Press.

Cox, R. (1997) 'Democracy in hard times: economic globalization and the limits to liberal democracy' in McGrew, A. (ed.) *The Transformation of Democracy*, Cambridge, Polity Press.

Crick, B. (2000) *In Defence of Politics* (5th edn), London, Continuum.

Dahl, R.A. (1961) *Who Governs? Democracy and Power in an American City*, New Haven, Yale University Press.

Danaher, G., Schirato, T. and Webb, J. (2000) *Understanding Foucault*, London, Sage.

Foucault, M. (1981) *The History of Sexuality: An Introduction*, Harmondsworth, Penguin.

Galbraith, J.K. (1986) 'Power and organization' in Lukes, S. (ed.) *Power*, Oxford, Blackwell.

Hague, R. and Harrop, M. (2001) *Comparative Government and Politics: An Introduction* (5th edn), Houndmills, Palgrave.

Hall, S. (1992) 'Introduction' in Hall, S. and Gieben, B. (eds) *Formations of Modernity*, Cambridge, Polity Press.

Hardt, M. and Negri, A. (2001) *Empire*, Cambridge, Harvard University Press.

Herz, N. (2002) *The Silent Takeover: Global Capitalism and the Death of Democracy*, London, Arrow Books.

Huysmans, J. (2005) *What is Politics?*, Edinburgh, Edinburgh University Press/The Open University.

Inglehart, R. (1997) *Modernization and Postmodernization: Cultural, Economic and Political Change in 43 Societies*, Princeton, Princeton University Press.

Kaase, M., Newton, K. and Scarborough, E. (1997) 'Beliefs in government', *Politics*, vol.17, no.2, pp.135–9.

Konrád, G. (1984) *Antipolitics*, London, Quartet Books.

Lukes, S. (1974) *Power: A Radical View*, London, Macmillan.

Lukes, S. (1986) 'Introduction' in Lukes, S. (ed.) *Power*, Oxford, Blackwell.

Mouffe, C. (1993) *The Return of the Political*, London, Verso.

The Observer (2002) London, 3 February.

Russell, B. (1960) *Power: A New Social Analysis*, London, Unwin.

Smith, S. (2002) 'L'Angola met fin à 27 années de guerre civile', *Le Monde*, Paris, 5 April.

Whiteley, P., Clarke, H., Sanders, D. and Stewart, M. (2001) 'The 2001 general election in Britain', *European Political Science*, autumn, vol.1, no.1, pp.34–40.

FURTHER READING

Crick, B. (2000) *In Defence of Politics* (5th edn), London, Continuum.

Paxman, J. (2003) *The Political Animal*, Harmondsworth, Penguin.

Poggi, G. (2001) *Forms of Power*, Cambridge, Polity.

Framing politics: the state in context

Bram Gieben and Paul Lewis

Contents

chapter 2

Centre & periphery

1 INTRODUCTION

As we saw in Chapter 1 the state is, arguably, now less prominent as a locus of power than it was a few decades ago and is not the prime sphere or centre of political activity that it was in the years immediately after the Second World War. Many people see the state as increasingly peripheral in a globalizing world in which it is challenged by alternative centres and networks of power. However, it is still the primary political unit with which many are concerned, and the framework within which – by one means or another – they engage or are affected by the political process. In this chapter we look at the different ways in which the state can be defined and how it has been studied. The various forms of contemporary democratic state are compared, and then different implications for democratic practice identified. In particular, we focus on the nature and role of the contemporary state, and look at the reasons why these are coming into question.

2 THE MODERN STATE IN QUESTION

The state is questioned in a variety of ways, largely due to the nature of the particular state in which people live. We know that states differ on a number of counts. They may be more or less powerful, large or small, strong or weak, rich or poor, stable or unstable, legitimate or illegitimate. A prominent distinction in contemporary politics is that between democratic states and those of a non-democratic nature, known as authoritarian. The democratization of states can generally be understood to bring them closer to the people, strengthen legitimacy and give them a more prominent role in contemporary political processes. But this does not always follow, and the increasingly democratic nature of the contemporary state has been accompanied by processes that increasingly place in question its central role.

Even the term 'state' itself is shot through with ambiguity, for instance, when describing states as modern or contemporary or nation-states (or sometimes all three together). Contemporary, for example, means the kind of state that exists now. The 'modern' state is that which existed in Europe from the early eighteenth century.

There has been a growing wave of democratization since the 1970s – given a major boost with the final collapse of Soviet power in 1991 – and the number of democratic states has indeed risen markedly. The US Freedom House

Foundation carries out an annual audit of the political dimensions of global democracy, which provides a convenient way of charting the democratization process. States are categorized as 'free', 'partly free' or 'not free' in terms of the political rights and civil liberties they offer to their citizens. The trend of democratization of states was clearly upwards in the last decade of the twentieth century (see Table 2.1). The actual number of democratic states also rose: from 117 out of a total of 191 in 1995–96 to 120 out of a total of 192 in 2000–01 (the actual numbers of democratic states referred to here include some states that, in the data in Table 2.1, were included under the category 'partly free' as well as those falling into the 'free' category).

TABLE 2.1   The global trend in the extension of political rights and civil liberties

	States						
	Free		Partly free		Not free		
Year	number	% of total	number	% of total	number	% of total	Total number
1990–91	65	39.4	50	30.3	50	30.3	165
1995–96	76	39.8	62	32.5	53	27.7	191
2000–01	86	44.8	58	30.2	48	25.0	192

Source: adapted from Karatnycky, 2001, p.7

When we talk of the process of democratization, the defining term is that of electoral democracy: a situation that includes competing parties, which have alternative programmes, have the ability to raise and use resources in their political campaigns and are able to contest free and fair elections. Of course, not all electoral democracies have a totally unblemished record in terms of political rights and civil liberties.

Apart from whether states are more or less 'democratic' in terms of their rights and liberties, the world of democratic states varies significantly in other respects. If democracy refers to 'people power' or (in slightly more specific terms) 'the rule of the people', both the nature of the people and that of their rule can be understood in very different ways. States may follow quite different courses when, for example, 'the people' disagree and have divergent preferences. Nevertheless, the democratic state, broadly understood, is one that provides the framework for much of contemporary political activity.

The ongoing process of 'democratization' has also been accompanied, rather paradoxically, by what may be termed the undermining or peripheralization of the state. It is unclear, as we have seen in Chapter 1, how far power can be understood to reside in the contemporary state – whether democratic or non-democratic. The application of the democratic category to many states in different parts of the world and the narrow focus on its electoral, procedural aspects also raises doubts about whether a rather 'thin' idea of democracy is being employed and one whose quality is often quite poor.

The political world shaped by this increasingly globalized form of democracy is also one characterized, as we saw in the previous chapter, by the people's suspicion of visible power centres and their doubts about the motives of those who act on their behalf. It generally has low levels of participation in established political institutions, and there is a growing perception that the claims of contemporary leaders to be politically authoritative are relatively weak, even in the more developed democracies.

Furthermore, the post-Cold War acceleration of democratization has explicitly involved the promotion of a 'democracy and market reform' package; that is, the building, in formerly non-democratic countries, of state structures which promote a base-line democracy and sustain the processes of economic globalization. It reflects a passive revolution that produces a limited democracy, lacks a secure base in an active civil society and provides a fragile basis for state structures and their operation (Cox, 1997, p.63).

Such doubts about the quality of contemporary democracy, as well as evidence of the mixed dynamics of global political change and the viability of modern states, all provide grounds for the further strengthening of the value shift identified by Inglehart (see Chapter 1). It is a value shift associated with the questioning of hierarchical structures and a growing tendency to reject their claims on how people should live their lives. The state is therefore increasingly brought into question by forces both inside and outside its borders.

There are other grounds on which the role of the contemporary state has been challenged. Forces on the periphery of the political system have often made claims on the power of the centre. Nations and other groups within established states have become more active, aspiring to greater autonomy and challenging from 'below' the state as the location of central power. At the end of the twentieth century, for example, the extensive empire of the Soviet Union broke up into its constituent parts. Of course, there were many drivers of this collapse, not least the failure of the Soviet command economy in its arms-driven competition with capitalism and the system's consequent loss of legitimacy, even among the elites who directed the state and controlled the Party.

However, what is interesting for our purposes is the drive for statehood in some of the former republics: their eagerness to proclaim sovereignty and reclaim their flag, culture and religious heritage. In Russia itself, a majority of a determined people in Chechnya continues to fight bitterly for independence. Meanwhile, in the old established nation-states such as the UK and Spain, some Scots and Welsh and Catalans and Basques also began to reassert their nationhood and demand that it be given political recognition in forms of devolution and autonomy – or all the way to independence in some cases. The advance of the Northern League indicates that the glue of state-sponsored nationalism also seems to be coming unstuck in a nation-state such as Italy (see Figure 2.1), which is relatively new in comparison with the longer established states of France or the UK.

FIGURE 2.1 Umberto Bossi, the populist leader of the Northern League, seen here with supporters at the source of the River Po, Italy, September 1996. The Northern League has vigorously campaigned for autonomy and, more recently, independence for regions in Northern Italy

It may be that the reassertion of these 'local nationalisms' in terms of the rights of the periphery can be explained by the relative decline of what the centralized nation-state can deliver for its sub-units. The northern Italians, smaller nations and other regional groupings may feel that they would be better off arguing their case, making alliances and grasping opportunities as small but vigorous units in a 'Europe of the regions', than continuing to throw in their lot with a traditional nation-state form that is often regarded as obsolete. What were once regarded as the peripheries of a central state system are now reasserting their political significance. It is not just the politicians who are unable to deliver on their promises, the state itself seems to be incapable of providing the outcomes expected of it.

This prompts a further question: is the nation-state still the most appropriate political unit for organizing human affairs in an increasingly interconnected world system? There are a number of threats from 'above', from other centres that render the state itself peripheral. One major question is associated with the dynamics of the world capitalist economy. The rise of multinational corporations with investment, factories and workforces in many countries is the most visible sign that economic production, ownership, trade and finance are now increasingly organized on an international basis. With the incorporation of the former Soviet Union and China into a world capitalist economic system, it is becoming increasingly hard for any state to operate independently of it.

Trillions of dollars are traded every day on the world's stock markets, all linked instantaneously by modern electronics. Investment capital has never been more mobile, and national governments have never been more vulnerable, to the decisions of these stock markets. Decisions taken by a democratically unaccountable elite of top managers from outside individual states, or simply the effects of the global market, can bankrupt or enrich parts of nations or even whole nations, as international flows of capital can mean investment in one place or withdrawal from another. In this sense, states themselves have taken on a peripheral status.

States have, of course, been engaged for centuries in international cooperation, treaties, short-term and long-term military alliances, economic cartels and global trade. The modern state has always been shaped by international forces. It is the unprecedented scale and acceleration of the various aspects of globalization that now cast doubt on the very notion of a government devising an independent national economic policy, or indeed of individual nation-states (even the largest) being fully able to control their own destiny. Even a contemporary 'hyperstate' such as the USA – the only one with any claim to global supremacy – has been shown to be vulnerable to terrorist attack by foreign forces.

In relation to this development, one further reason for the state now being placed in question is that many of the political problems arising in the modern world are not ones that the traditional centralized nation-state is well equipped to tackle alone. Some of the most urgent problems we face – environmental pollution, the global traffic in illicit drugs, illegal immigration and security against terrorist attack – are obviously transnational in character and, equally obviously, exceed the power of any one state to solve, even within its own borders. Coordinated action in and across states is essential if these problems are to be tackled at all.

All of these developments place the state in question and challenge its traditionally central role in most political worlds of modern times.

SUMMARY

- The increasing global prevalence of the democratic state has been accompanied by growing doubts about the contemporary role of the state and the quality of the democracy it embodies.

- States are challenged from below by internal local nationalisms and from above by the workings of the global economy and the growing importance of transnational problems.

3 STUDYING AND DEFINING THE MODERN STATE

In the previous chapter the relation between politics and power was sketched out. We saw that if we are interested in the location and exercise of power in any given society we must study the state, because it is still in many ways the dominant focus of power and authority, or at least the dominant form through which power is exercised. The role and centrality of the contemporary state may well be open to question, but its historical significance and continuing importance in contemporary political analysis and practice can hardly be doubted. What, precisely, is involved in the study of the state deserves, therefore, closer analysis.

The history of the last 150 years in the West has been a history of extraordinary growth in the size and reach of the modern state. In many countries the state became the largest employer. In 1979 in the UK more than 40 per cent of adults depended upon the state for their primary income, although numbers have since declined. Progressively, the modern, centralized, bureaucratic state expanded its scale of operation, taking on more and more responsibility to fund, run or simply regulate and support activities once considered just private.

State power is exercised through an enormous range of institutions: legal, administrative and educational, and even reaches into what were once considered the most private of areas. Sex is regulated by legislation on the age of consent. Birth is closely regulated in hospitals and through stringent conditions for applying to give birth at home. Education is compulsory, and its quality is tightly overseen by the state. Both marriage and death have to be formalized and registered. The quality of such essentials of life as air and water are regulated by the state. Thought may be free, but its expression is controlled by laws on censorship, slander, libel, blasphemy and public order.

Work is the subject of a host of regulations on the conditions under which employers and employed contract with each other. The state has the power to take away your money (taxation and fines), your freedom to travel abroad (passport), your right to strike (by legislation or sending in troops), your children (custody and access), your liberty (jail) and, in some states, your life itself (execution). It can declare war without your approval, conscript you against your principles, order you into battle in conditions which are suicidal, and shoot you for desertion if you refuse to go over the top.

When reading about the decline of the UK and the erosion of the power of the state by globalization, international economic forces and so on, we also need to bear in mind that the British state still has the power to devastate cities of the former Soviet Union or those of other countries in a unilateral nuclear attack. Quite a bit of power left, then.

You are probably now reasonably convinced that questions about the state are indeed central to many of the most important discussions about politics and power in modern Britain and the different worlds of contemporary politics – even if they do not cover the whole story. When you move from everyday conversations about politics to academic, in our case social scientific, discussions of issues like these you require a more careful use of terms. You need to probe into the use of words and the meaning of concepts or ideas. A better and more elaborate toolkit is needed to carry out more careful and detailed work on contemporary and comparative politics. In setting out to answer almost any essay or examination question, you are going to have to define your terms, and the first thing the careful student discovers is that most terms have a number of different – though usually overlapping – meanings. Teasing these out brings a deeper understanding, and enables you to give more subtle, thoughtful and impressive answers.

We need to move on, then, to questions of definition. Careful readers may already have spotted that the word 'state' is actually being used in rather different ways in the questions above. So, let's tease out some common usages. People actually use the word 'state' to mean:

1   A country's major political *institutions* controlled by its current government.

2   A country's *regime*, or the particular kind of political order that prevails.

3   A *nation* – a more or less culturally homogeneous group of people living in a particular place. Calling an entity a 'nation-state' draws attention to the fact that such a group has its own state or that, in a sense, it rules itself. This is generally what we mean when we refer to a 'country'. With the rise of more culturally and ethnically diverse countries, some observers today refer to 'multinational' states.

4   The *sub-units* within a larger, federal state entity (such as the USA or the former USSR), which retain a large measure of local autonomy but hand over to a higher level some major functions such as defence or foreign policy.

Let's go through these.

The first notion of the state is one of the most common, but in this context it is particularly important to distinguish state from government: for example, when a government goes out of office all the institutions of the state – parliament, monarchy, army, police, civil servants, health service and school system – remain intact. The second concept of regime is rather broader and refers to how the political sphere is ordered – whether, for example, it is democratic rule or authoritarian rule which prevails.

When we talk of nation-states losing their power to multinational corporations, we are generally combining senses (1) and (3). A problem with (3), however, is that there are homogeneous cultural groups – for example the Kurds – which are geographically concentrated but politically separated among three or more states. Some of the fiercest battles in history have been waged by self-styled nations seeking to achieve their own state.

Finally, I think most of us are aware that when we talk about states in sense (4) we are talking about entities that resemble fully fledged states in some ways (having defined geographical boundaries, legislatures and some tax-raising powers), but which are located within an overall federal system and lack the full authority and resources of the nation-state. Unitary states such as the UK and France should therefore be distinguished from federal states such as the USA and Germany, where the minor, constituent 'state' units have clearly defined, but limited, powers. Most of us would therefore be very surprised to hear, say, that California had declared war on Mexico – even though California's GNP would be one of the highest in the world if it were an independent nation-state.

Of course, the understandings above do overlap somewhat. Very commonly, when we talk of a state doing something internationally, we mean something like: the government of a particular territory, claiming to represent the people of that territory, using its control of 'the apparatus of rule' to act. This also combines (1) and (3). When reading about the state, in this book and elsewhere, you will find references to all these conceptions, and you must always be alert to which sense or meaning is being used in a particular context.

To further our discussions, we clearly need a working definition of the state. David Held (1992, p.87) offers this definition for modern states as institutional entities: 'Political apparatuses, distinct from both ruler and ruled, with supreme jurisdiction over a demarcated territorial area, backed up by a claim to a monopoly of coercive power, and enjoying a minimum level of support or loyalty from their citizens.'

This is a concise and useful definition, from which we can pick up some helpful insights. It primarily refers to meaning (1) identified above, but carries some overtones of (2) and (3) in terms of the level of support or loyalty it can command. Let's now examine its major implications.

Political apparatuses
These refer to the structures of administration and government that provide the means of political rule and implement government decisions.

Distinct from both ruler and ruled
States in this sense are modern creations. Nation-states were formed by a set of processes which gathered momentum in about the seventeenth century, as we shall see in Section 5. In pre-democratic states absolute monarchs could legitimately say, as Louis XIV famously did, *L'état, c'est moi*. In one sense this 'Sun King' was right in that he was at the apex of a social and political system of authority. Yet neither the monarchy nor its administrative apparatus died with him. The separation of the authority of the state from particular individuals and families, often claiming a divine sanction for their rule, was one of the major stages in the emergence of the modern state.

FIGURE 2.2 The Queen reading her speech at the State Opening of Parliament, House of Lords, October 1996. Each year, the speech is written for her by the Prime Minister and government of the day

Supreme jurisdiction

An absolutely central fact about the state is its claim to *sovereignty*. This is a core concept in political science and the law. There are scholarly debates about its meaning, its application, and its reality or capacity to be realized in given circumstances. However, for our present purposes it is sufficient to define the state as a supreme law-making power. An institution defined as sovereign recognizes no higher authority, and there is no appeal from its edicts. In the UK, the sovereign power is accepted to be that of 'the Queen in Parliament', although in practice the political power of the monarch is now almost entirely formal (Figure 2.2).

A demarcated territorial area

Earlier political systems, such as those of the ancient empires (Persia, Rome and China), had less clearly defined boundaries. It is also worth noting that the growing emphasis on territorial control which accompanied the rise of modern states had important implications for the populations they contained. The people within state borders do not always comprise homogeneous populations with a single language or culture. Modern states were formed by a process of unification and they vigorously attempted to impose a unitary culture, though not always with complete success.

A monopoly of the legitimate use of coercion

This means a monopoly within the state's territorial boundaries. The relation between the state and violence, or war, is absolutely crucial, and it has several dimensions. It is a commonly held view that all states have their origins in war. Certainly, if they lack the physical force to defend themselves, they may not remain independent states for very long. Second, no state can tolerate for long a group of its citizens perpetuating violence in the pursuit of their own particular aims, or refusing to accept the authority of the state and its laws. You need to be aware that for a sovereign power to have such a monopoly requires a society that is largely pacified and orderly; it also implies that in the event of disorder the state possesses, and will deploy, the overwhelming force necessary to reimpose order. To say, for example, that some parts of Belfast are or have been no-go areas would reflect a serious challenge to the authority and effectiveness of the British state (Figure 2.3).

A minimum level of support or loyalty

This refers to the characteristic that the influential German sociologist, Max Weber (1964, pp.324–9), called *legitimacy,* and which he took to be central to the very character of the state. By legitimacy he meant that there must be a belief in the minds of its citizens that the dominion of the state is morally right or justified. No state, he believed, can maintain its power and continue over

FIGURE 2.3   A 'no-go' cartoon, which appeared in the *Daily Telegraph* in May 1972

time through the use of force alone. The state's citizens must feel that the state is lawfully established and rules at least partly in their interests. Weber set out the following three different grounds on which such legitimacy might rest.

Tradition
The form of the state has been recognized and accepted from time immemorial. It is sanctified by tradition, and usually claims to rule according to custom.

Charisma
The authority of the state depends upon the personality of a single dominant individual. A great leader may rise to power, especially at times of enormous historical change, such as war or revolution, and come to personify the state for a generation of individuals. Hitler, Mussolini and Stalin were the major examples of the twentieth century. Ghaddafi (in Libya) or Saddam Hussein (in Iraq, until 2003) are more recent examples. One problem with this form of legitimation is that the legitimacy of the state can dissolve with the death of the leader. When the leader dies the transition to the next stage is likely to be turbulent.

Legal–rational
Legitimacy here depends on the ruler(s) having gone through a prescribed procedure laid down by law (such as winning an election). This is the most common form of legitimacy in contemporary advanced states, and underlies the increasing prevalence of democratic regimes. By the way, Hitler's legitimacy in Germany was at first also legal–rational: in 1933 his party won the largest number of seats in elections to the Bundestag (the German Parliament). One could argue that this rule later became charismatic, and that this was one reason why the Nazi state perished with him.

Having illuminated these sources for state legitimacy, Weber then somewhat casually remarks that in fact most citizens obey the state from a robust mixture of hope and fear.

The final thing to be said about legitimacy at this stage is that all states tend to work hard at manufacturing or retaining their legitimacy. The excellence or moral superiority of a particular system of rule (for example democracy and free markets) are 'sold' very hard to the population, opposing systems (for example communism or religious autocracies) are systematically deprecated, and states of all kinds equally lay claim to be representing the will of the people.

You should now have a clearer view of what is meant by the state in the commonest sense as outlined in (1) above; that is, the state as a set of institutions controlling a given territory. Next, we need to take a wider look at the context in which the modern state operates.

SUMMARY

- The state remains a major political arena and framework for much of contemporary political life.
- In order to study it, we need to distinguish the four different ways in which the term is often used.
- It is also essential to acquaint ourselves with a satisfactory working definition of the state and to understand the terms that are involved in this.

4 THE MODERN STATE AND ITS ENVIRONMENT

The modern state finds itself on the border of two different worlds – it faces both inwards and outwards, and the way it interacts with these worlds helps determine where it is located on the map of centre/periphery relations. It appears as actor as well as the focus of others acting upon it.

Facing inwards, the state engages with its own society. It is useful to envisage this in terms of a relation between the state and civil society, and to express the difference between them in terms of the public and the private sectors.

- The public sector in modern Britain would include all those institutions that make up the state or are directly owned, controlled or financed by it. That would include parliament, the monarchy, the army and police forces, the civil service, nationalized industries, the courts, most schools and hospitals, local government, the Inland Revenue, and so forth.

- The private sector of civil society, by contrast, means all those social movements, institutions and activities not directly owned and regulated by the state: the family, private businesses, lands, charities, clubs and associations of all kinds which organize and fund themselves according to the needs and wishes of private individuals or groups.

However, the boundary between the public and the private is not that clear-cut. Many public–private relations are not either/or issues but are matters of degree. This brings us to two very important points.

1 Both the state and civil society are products of history, of human action, and are subject to continual change. There is nothing fixed or inevitable about the form of the state, about the extent and character of civil society, or of the relations between them. It follows that the boundary between them, the balance between public and private in any given society, will always be shifting and somewhat indistinct.

2 The nature of those changes will depend upon social and political struggles; and those in turn will depend upon *ideas* – the ideas held by the individuals and groups concerned about what the state is, and what it ought to be.

We can see, then, that the state faces inwards as it rules over and engages at all levels with its civil society, and that this civil society will play its own part in forming that state and determining how it works.

But what does the state do when it looks outwards? What is the form of international society in which it is enmeshed? Is the state a central or peripheral force on the broader stage? A traditional way to think about this is to envisage the state as an actor in an international society of nation-states. We will see that this international society is very different from a national society.

First, unlike national or domestic law, international law is poorly developed, and there are often no effective and authoritative law-making and law-enforcing mechanisms. Resolutions of the United Nations are often not implemented, and the European Union relies on the administration of its member states to enforce its decisions. Since every state considers itself, by definition, to be sovereign, it does not accord legitimacy to any body above itself, nor does it give up the right to use violence in pursuit of its own ends. That doesn't mean that violence is the normal or even most frequent mode of interaction between states. In order to pursue their interests, states form political and military alliances, engage in complex interlinking patterns of trade, jointly attempt to tackle common problems (drug trafficking or pollution, for example), and accept obligations and restrictions of all kinds. In short, international state action in both the political and economic arenas is marked overwhelmingly by negotiation and cooperation.

A second aspect of the international dimension to the state and its activities is this: there are many actors on the world stage other than states, and some of them are major players. They range in size and power from regional blocs such as the EU and security groupings such as the North Atlantic Treaty Organization, to economic multinational corporations (MNCs) and other non-governmental organizations (NGOs), to more specialized smaller groupings such as Greenpeace and the World Council of Churches. States engage internationally, then – and not just unilaterally with each other but multilaterally as part of large transnational groupings and at all sorts of levels with smaller and more diffuse actors.

Deciding upon the status and nature of some transnational actors and how to engage with them can be a major problem. Consider in this context the nature of relations between al-Qaeda and the USA. The USA interpreted 11 September 2001 as a war-like attack on its territory and al-Qaeda as an organized belligerent. Others analysing the situation understood the terrorists to be part of a loose global network – and that its informal dispersed form of organization lay at the root of its effectiveness and particularly threatening nature.

Important questions of perception and definition are involved here. By looking at the activity of the state both domestically and internationally, however, a rounded picture begins to emerge of the state in action. You can begin to see that the state stands at the intersection of two different 'worlds', the national and the international. The state is shaped by its engagement with forces in both domains.

There is also a third, inner 'world' to which political scientists must pay attention. It is the world of the state itself: the actors, processes and powers *within* the 'apparatus of rule'. It is clear that the state itself can be an actor. It can pass a law internally and enforce it. It can also act unilaterally or in concert with others internationally, for example by declaring war and joining a military expedition. Yet it is important to grasp that the state itself is also *the object of political action and a site of struggle*. What does this mean? We have established that the state represents an enormous concentration of power, and a focal point of political action in modern societies. Revolutionaries seek to overthrow regimes, and parties seek to win elections, in order to control the state. Interest and pressure groups lobby the state (whichever party is in power) in order to influence its policy. And they do so to bring about political change, but in all cases the engine of political change must be the state.

Therefore, the state itself can be a site of struggle. If we take the business of politics to be the competition, more or less orderly or rule-governed, between entities such as classes, parties, or individuals for competitive advantage, it is obvious that they must focus their efforts on the seat of power. When we talked about the difference between state and government, we spoke of the government gaining control of the 'apparatus of rule' for a given period. This way of talking is a kind of shorthand, and the problem with this is that this model of the state is misleading. The state is modelled as a kind of machine: to get where you want to go, all that's needed is to get into the driving seat. In reality, the state is far more complicated than that.

The machinery of the state is vast, and is made up of many different component parts and sets of individuals, each of whom may have their own interests and their own view of the world, their own values and priorities. Fans of the TV series *Yes Minister* (which was, apparently, one of Margaret Thatcher's favourite programmes) will remember how the minister, committed to the government's election promises to reduce waste, cut red tape and minimize bureaucracy, was systematically thwarted by Sir Humphrey, the civil service mandarin elegantly protecting his own interests and those of the civil service (Figure 2.4). Similarly, different departments can disagree over priorities: for example, the Foreign Office may disagree with the Home Office, and the Treasury with all the spending departments. One policy can work against another: for example, the Conservative Government in the UK in office from 1979 to 1997 believed in cutting public spending and in 'making industry leaner and fitter'. The means employed to achieve the latter, however, had the effect of putting thousands more on to the register of those receiving unemployment benefit. This increased public spending, as well as the numbers of civil servants required.

Much academic effort has gone into analysing 'what kind of animal' the state is, or how to conceptualize it, and there has been much careful empirical analysis of how it works, for example, how policy is actually made in a particular area. It is obviously inadequate to think of the state simply as a kind of black box, which receives inputs at one end and produces outputs in a

FIGURE 2.4   The Rt. Hon. James Hacker, MP, Minister for Administrative Affairs, whose work is closely overseen by his under-secreatary, Sir Humphrey Appleby, and his Private Secretary, Bernard Wooley – a scene from *Yes Minister*

predictable way at the other. It is more like a complex organism that is: capable of shaping incoming representations and demands; able to advance – overtly or covertly – its own interests and values; and works according to a logic (or logics) of its own.

SUMMARY

- The state faces 'inwards' towards civil society. The relations between the two are subject to constant negotiation and renegotiation.
- The state also faces 'outwards' towards the international community and its diverse actors.
- There is another arena of state activity: its inner life and its existence as a site of political activity and contestation in its own right.

5   THE RISE OF THE MODERN STATE

A long historical view serves to underline the wide-ranging political forms that have existed: the Greek city-state or *polis*; early Germanic 'clan' societies based on communal modes of production and ruled by tiered councils of aristocrats, warriors and popular assemblies; the sprawling Greek, Roman and Holy Roman empires, which more or less successfully claimed authority over enormous numbers of large and small cultures and territories; feudalism with its extremely complex system of overlapping ties and obligations, which eventually fragmented power until it became increasingly personal and local in focus; the highly sophisticated medieval Italian city-states; and monarchies with varying degrees of reliance on other bodies representing powerful social groups, such as the nobility and the clergy. Standing alongside all these shifts and struggles in the realm of secular power was the Church, which over many centuries asserted its own claim to power, authority and obedience.

However, the dominant kind of political system and early state form that preceded the modern nation-state in Europe from about the sixteenth century was the absolute monarchy form or states that approximated to this model. From this time a number of historical processes combined to shape a more recognizable, modern state which emerged as the powerful centre of political life across much of the globe (see Chapter 1, Box 1.1). Individual monarchs, once precariously juggling relations with powerful nobles, gradually won the battle for power and authority over all other sources of authority. Smaller and weaker territories were incorporated into larger and stronger ones. The decline of feudalism meant the end of serfdom and of feudal obligations such as military service to one's feudal superior. These were replaced by money rents, and by a standing army paid for by an early form of national taxation.

Absolute states, like all states, were expansionist; their capacity to make war depended on being able to pay for it, and that depended on having a strong economy. In the long transition from feudalism to capitalism, trade and commerce were already expanding, and the absolute monarchs set about removing all the old feudal practices – such as local taxation, toll-gates, banditry or poor communications – that were impediments to an efficient national market.

In this way, the expansion of commerce and communications undermined the dense local structures of feudalism, and the landed nobility who were their beneficiaries, as trade, security, law and administration began to take place on a national stage within increasingly fixed boundaries. Taken together, these developments signified the introduction of more unitary and effective rule and a progressive concentration of power into, or under the control of, a single sovereign authority. Needless to say, this increasing volume of state activity necessitated a marked increase in the number of civil servants: 'linked to the court there developed a new administrative apparatus involving the beginnings of a permanent, professional bureaucracy' (Mann, 1988, p.476).

Externally, a new pattern of inter-state relations began to emerge. Trade relations with other states began to increase, and again absolute rulers actively sought to further their national economic interests, with military help and protectionism, as prescribed by the prevailing orthodoxy in economics: mercantilism. The absolutist states also began to formalize the relations between themselves and new diplomatic institutions. In these absolutist states we can see the beginnings of a modern international system of states.

By means of these new methods, judiciously balanced with the traditional instruments of war, strategic alliances and royal intermarriage, an initially small number of sovereign states engaged in what Poggi (1978, p.60) has called 'an open-ended, competitive and risk-laden power struggle'. The winners in this struggle were the new form of nation-state and this gradually became the dominant form of state, at first in Europe and then, over the last 200 years, in the world. It became the norm for every substantial body of people who felt themselves distinguished from others by race, tradition, culture and language to desire their own nation-state.

This prompts the question: why, of all the many forms of state and polity afforded us by history, has this particular form become so successful? The answer, according to Held (1992), is that in a hostile world the state was the form which most successfully assembled and deployed the means of making war. Some of the key organizations of the modern state emerged at the intersection of warfare and the attempt to pay for it: 'it was the increasing scale of war ... as well as its increasing reliance on technological change, industrialization and specialization, which, in combination with the growth of commercial, legal and diplomatic relations between states, gave the modern centralized ... state its "distinctive edge" over other state forms' (Held, 1992, pp.95–6).

This forging of the modern nation-state in the crucible of war and preparation for war had one more momentous effect. All states depend for their existence on extracting resources from their societies, but the greater demands of the nation-state in this area gave its citizenry some leverage over their rulers, some bargaining power with dominant political groups.

It was therefore understandable that the more costly and demanding war became, the more the rulers had to bargain for and win the support of their subjects. As people became increasingly drawn into war preparations, the more they became aware of being members of a political community – and of the rights and obligations such membership might confer. In this way the expansion of citizenship, or membership of an inclusive political community, was closely tied in with the military and administrative requirements of the state. The tightly meshed organization of the modern state, and the politicization of social relations and everyday activities it involved, was very much a consequence of modern warfare and the preparations made for it which followed in its wake. The gradual formation of representative and democratic political institutions was a paradoxical outcome of this process (Held, 1992, p.98).

Before we leave the subject of the relationship between war and the modern state, we need to make three more points.

- First, the fact that the early state was dependent for its success on developing and amassing the resources to wage war is also regarded by some writers as a crucial stage in its development. This is because it involved a novel process of intervention in the liberal economy, a process which was to lead all the way to the twentieth-century commitment to 'managed capitalism'.

- Second, the boundaries of modern European states were determined by the results of wars over many centuries. To take a recent example: if the outcome of the Second World War had been different, then the state boundaries might look very different today.

- Finally, it is undoubtedly true that the experience of centralized planning and active direction of the nation's resources, especially in the Second World War, profoundly altered dominant perceptions of what the state could and should do in its pursuit of peacetime goals such as full employment.

However, as the nation-state became the dominant form of the state in Europe, its character was shaped also by profound social and economic developments. History offers scarcely any example of a group or class possessed of great wealth (economic power) which did not seek to translate this into political power. With the rise of the manufacturing and commercial middle classes in the seventeenth and eighteenth centuries, absolute monarchs had to bargain with them to an increasing extent concerning representation and political influence – the Glorious Revolution in England (1688–89, which resulted in the beginnings of parliamentary supremacy and King James II being deposed) was only one example of a more general process. This reflected the changing balance of class forces in which the so-called 'constitutional state' emerged. It was not yet democratic, but it did embody a regime which limited and qualified the rights of the monarchy in the name of individual rights of citizens. At first that select group comprised only wealthy male property holders, but a century of popular struggle lead incrementally to universal adult suffrage (although in France women had to wait until 1944 and, in Italy, until 1945). By the middle of the twentieth century, universal suffrage existed in almost all European states, with the exception of Switzerland.

Democratization was just one of the enormous forces which combined to transform traditional, overwhelmingly rural societies into a recognizably modern state form. Nationalism, industrialization and urbanization all played their parts. There are many forms of nationalism, but within the territory of the nation-state there emerged one of the most significant. This was a systematic attempt by the rulers to inculcate a sense of community, of common identity, among the often diverse religions and ethnic groups within their borders. Of course, going to war against a foreign enemy has a way of uniting previously discordant factions at home and, if successful, of improving the popularity of a given state, but there were other ways of building a nation. We can identify just a few of many historical examples from the UK. After the final defeat of Jacobinism at Culloden in 1746, the British state suppressed the wearing of the kilt and the speaking of Gaelic in the Highlands of Scotland. During the next century national newspapers proliferated and gave their readers accounts of imperial conquests, which helped develop a heightened sense of national identity. At the same time improvements in transport and the mass production of manufactured goods in the course of industrialization lead to an increasing standardization of consumption patterns.

These were to be followed decades later by national radio and television broadcasting, which had a profound effect in further homogenizing the national political culture. Put simply, the differences between Orcadians (inhabitants of the Orkney Islands) and the Cornish are reduced if they all watch the same news, talk about the same soap operas, and purchase the same consumer durables. State rituals such as the investiture of the Prince of Wales, royal weddings and funerals, and the monarch's broadcast to the 'family' of subjects, were all conscious attempts to create and reinforce the feeling of national unity, of belonging. It is not so long ago, too, that references to the (white) citizens of the Commonwealth were made in terms of 'kith and kin'.

The rise of capitalism and the process of industrialization also brought in their wake two new social classes, those whom Karl Marx called the bourgeoisie and the proletariat. The former comprised the manufacturing and commercial entrepreneurs and their financial counterparts, who first rivalled – and then overtook – in wealth and political influence the traditional landed aristocracy. The second new group, the proletariat, was the urban industrial working class, whose struggles for trade union and political rights profoundly altered the landscape of politics and the character of the state.

The consequences of all these forces working together was, over the hundred years from about 1815 to 1915, a transformation of the state from a small set of institutions and individuals, principally concerned to extract resources from the population and spend them on the maintenance and deployment of armed forces, to an ever expanding machinery of government. State expenditure grew massively. In 1760 the British central state spent 18 million pounds, and in 1911 almost 160 million. A similar eightfold increase took place in France, while state expenditure in Austria, Prussia–Germany and the USA rose even more rapidly (Mann, 1993, p.362).

Economic growth, of course, was one major factor that made this possible, while inflation made the real rise in expenditure less precipitous. There was also significant population growth, which affected both sides of the equation and occurred at different rates in the leading states. This made patterns of per capita state expenditure in constant prices show a rather different picture, but there has still been a very major rise over time (Table 2.2). Between 1820 and 1910, on the eve of the First World War, state expenditure per head of population grew significantly – although more in some countries than others. The rate of growth was highest in the USA, where a whole new state had to be constructed once independence was gained from Great Britain, and was lowest in Britain itself which was long resistant to the idea of the big state and an extensive administration.

TABLE 2.2   Trends in per capita state expenditure in constant prices[1]

Year	France (central only)	Great Britain	USA	Germany	Austria (central only)
1820	27	50	8	–	19
1830	31	48	8	–	14
1840	35	42	13	32	19
1850	43	53	14	46	25
1860	50	57	18	44	25
1870	67	50	35	83	35
1880	85	67	37	48	41
1890	92	63	51	66	54
1900	99	118	80	86	72
1910	100	100	100	100	100

[1]Constant prices are shown relative to a benchmark of 100 for the year 1910
Source: Mann, 1993, p.365

The form of modern state that this pattern of development constructed was one which progressively extended its reach into the private sphere, in particular by intervening in the free market to regulate industrial capitalism. It progressively expanded the public sphere by accepting an obligation to provide some of the essentials of a civilized life through public action in fields such as health and education. In doing so, it also greatly increased its capacity for surveillance and the control of its population. One good way to characterize the expanding public sector in Britain from the early nineteenth to the late twentieth century is to say that matters such as sanitation, education and pensions, formerly not considered the responsibility of the state, gradually became the objects of political action. The state did not just become the dominant centre of political life, its power and influence permeated society and impinged on virtually all sectors of the periphery of the political system.

Seen in that way, the coming of the welfare state, and all the taxation and regulation that accompanied it, could be seen to enlarge the scope of state action, and the realm of the political more generally. Much of this enlargement was fought for. It was also resisted by the more reactionary conservative forces who opposed the rise of a powerful state on the grounds that it threatened their traditional rights and liberties, and it increased the amount of tax they had to pay. Others saw the benefits, both national and international, of a larger, more powerful and inclusive state. It has also been suggested that the reason why Britain never had a revolution was that its conservatives perceived that their interests would be best served by making concessions to popular demands and granting measures of reform – that they knew when to bend in order not to break.

Bobbio (1987) has written about the way in which democratization and the growth of the welfare state went hand in hand (Box 2.1). T.H. Marshall presented a view of a similar process in terms of citizenship and rights. He

---

BOX 2.1   **Democratization and the welfare state**

The reasons why democratization should have gone hand in hand with bureaucratization, which is after all something Max Weber clearly envisaged, are generally understood. When those who had the right to vote were just property owners, it was natural that they should ask the public authority to perform a single basic function – the protection of private property. This gave rise to the doctrine of the limited state, the night watchman state, or, as it is now known, the minimal state ... from the moment the vote was extended to the illiterate it was inevitable that they would ask the state to set up free schools, and so take on board a responsibility unknown to the state of traditional oligarchies and of the first bourgeois oligarchy. When the right to vote was also extended to non-property owners, to the have-nots, to those whose only property was their labour, it resulted in them asking for state protection from unemployment, and in due course for state insurance schemes against illness and old age, for maternity benefits, for subsidized housing, etc. So it was that the welfare state came about, like it or not, as the response to demands emanating from below, demands which were, in the fullest sense of the word, democratic.

(Bobbio, 1987, p.38)

spoke of the expansion in the meaning, and indeed the benefits, of citizenship as being in three parts or phases – civil, political and social – and all such rights being linked with membership of a modern welfare state and capable of being exercised through it (see Chapter 4).

On the basis of these developments, moreover, we can chart the emergence of the dominant form of contemporary state, the modern state of liberal democracy. We have seen that the principal activity of the early modern nation-state was in extracting resources from its population in order to make war. With the extension of the franchise, it gradually assumed responsibility for providing a certain minimum standard of material welfare and security to all its citizens (see Figure 2.5). During the twentieth century the proportion of state budgets devoted to military spending has steadily decreased in relation to non-military expenditures. However, the striking growth of welfare provision, in both absolute and relative terms, emphatically does not mean that state spending on the armed forces, or the role of the military in society and the economy, has been reduced to relative insignificance. The 'civilianization' of government has been accompanied by the 'militarization'

FIGURE 2.5 This cartoon appeared in the *Daily Mail* in early December 1942, following the publication of the Beveridge Report a month earlier, which laid the foundations for the establishment of the post-war welfare state

of society (McGrew, 1992a, p.77). The 'war on terror' that emerged after '9–11' is a continuing reflection of this development, and there are good reasons to believe that the rulers of many modern states find it helpful to operate in some kind of war climate (be it 'cold' or 'hot').

SUMMARY

- The beginnings of the modern state can be traced back to the sixteenth century and the rise of the absolute state.
- War was a key factor in fostering the development of the modern state and enlarging its power over society.
- Industrialization, urbanization, nationalism and democratization were all processes which combined to form the advanced capitalist state that emerged in the twentieth century.

6 THE VARIETY OF STATE FORMS

In making this range of definitional, historical and conceptual points, we have assumed that the features of the modern state are sufficiently generalized to enable us to make useful explanatory remarks about it. In reality, contemporary states exhibit a variety of specific forms. There are numerous ways of distinguishing between the different forms, including, of course, important contrasts that can be drawn between established democracies and the many dictatorships and other forms of authoritarian rule that still exist in the contemporary world.

Those under some kind of authoritarian rule numbered 75, or 39 per cent of the total, in 2000, according to the survey reported in Section 1 (bear in mind that, in Table 2.1, some partly free states will be included under authoritarian rule). They included the few remaining communist states of Cuba, North Korea and Vietnam, as well as the politically vigorous and economically thriving state of China, military regimes such as Burma, authoritarian monarchies such as Saudi Arabia, together with a substantial number of more straightforward dictatorships. In real life politics, of course, things are not fixed, and some of these states show a mix of characteristics and a composite political form, and could be placed in more than one category.

In addition, there are, or have been, a number of so-called 'failed' states, many of which are in Africa, including Somalia, the Congo, Liberia and Sierra Leone, as well as Bosnia in the former Yugoslavia. What constitutes a failure is often a matter of opinion or value judgement, but in terms of state forms it might simply refer to political entities that fail to embody the criteria of statehood spelt out in Section 2; for example, they are not sovereign and cannot maintain a monopoly of the legitimate use of coercion within their boundaries.

Indeed, it is often argued that the most critical feature of the modern state is its high political capacity: what 'enables the state as an institution not just to survive and carry out rudimentary functions, but to make and implement policies throughout the territory over which it claims sovereignty' (Gill, 2003, p.ix). Underlying this characteristic is the state's ability to marshal a substantial amount of 'infrastructural' power rather than having to rely on more traditional forms of despotic power. In this context infrastructural power means the sum of resources the state can successfully call upon and deploy in order to 'penetrate its territories and logistically implement decisions'. It is a collective power, 'power through society', which coordinates social life through state infrastructures (Mann, 1993, p.59). This is the capacity that the modern state – uniquely – has been able to develop and which underlies the contemporary dominance of the capitalist state in its prevalent liberal-democratic form.

However, this still leaves us with a wide variety of contemporary state forms. Even if we confine ourselves to the advanced capitalist states we are confronted with a broad variety. Multi-party liberal democracies vary in their constitutional arrangements, political structures, welfare, health and education systems, and of course in the extent of their economic and political power. In terms of constitutional structure, the UK, France and Japan are unitary states, while the USA and Germany have a federal structure. The UK and Japan have parliamentary systems of government, for example, while Finland and the USA have a presidential form. Many Western European states, in particular the Scandinavian countries, have a comprehensive welfare regime while others, such as the USA, have more limited state welfare provision.

We have brought our discussion of the rise of the modern state to a close by directing attention to its progressive democratization and the accompanying rise of the welfare state. This, though, is rather a general view to be taking at the beginning of the twenty-first century: a time when the fate of the welfare state has been under discussion and considerable threat for a couple of decades, and while scepticism grows about the effectiveness of modern democratic practice as post-materialist values take root in many societies (Chapter 1). New social movements, such as those concerned with environmentalism or the anti-globalization campaign, confront the state with novel challenges and bring specific interests to the fore which demand new avenues of representation.

Contemporary democratic states may become increasingly differentiated in how they cope with such challenges and the nature of the structural response they make to such changes in the character of the social and political environment. Distinctions can be drawn between established liberal democracies in terms of the response they make to new social interests. First, these states may become more inclusive or exclusive with respect to representation within the state. Second, they may show an active or passive response towards who gets represented. States can therefore be classified according to how they score on these two dimensions and major Western democracies differentiated by their response to the emergence of new interests (Table 2.3).

TABLE 2.3   Classifying contemporary states

	Inclusive	Exclusive
Passive	pluralism: USA	legal corporatism: Germany
Active	expansive corporatism: Norway	authoritarian liberalism: UK (post-1979)

Source: Dryzek *et al.*, 2002, p.660

The importance of the passive–active state distinction and of the state's stance towards new interests, whether inclusive or exclusive, can be demonstrated by looking at some examples. The USA is a good example of a passively inclusive state whose pluralism does little to put obstacles in the way of social movements becoming organized and forming interest groups to lobby government. Such groups can therefore lobby legislatures and administrative agencies, as well as form parties to contest and possibly win seats in elections. The state does not do much to help them, though.

Norway, on the other hand, has an actively inclusive state which organizes the concerns that in other countries might provide the impetus for social movements to form in civil society. There is a clear pay-off for the state in this situation as potentially oppositional groups are, as a result, likely to moderate their demands in exchange for official funds and access to participation in policy making (Dryzek *et al.*, 2002, p.669).

We can see the outcomes of exclusive responses in the cases of Germany and the UK. A clear case of passive exclusion can be seen in Germany, where there is a high level of administrative secrecy and a legalistic, unitary conception of the public interest, which sees opposition as an illegitimate obstruction to the performance of official duty. This is characterized as legal corporatism. Social movements, such as the one for environmental protection, which emerged in the early 1970s, were thus thrown back on their own resources and developed as participatory and independent citizens' groups. Despite the politically unfavourable image such a state conjures up in terms of passive exclusion, Germany has in fact provided the most conducive environment of the four types (shown in Table 2.3) for contemporary environmentalism to develop. It has thus achieved a high level of ecological modernization (the efficient use of resources and capacity to deal with pollution problems, thus encouraging a more sustainable form of capitalism) and a vigorous sphere of 'subpolitics' (Dryzek *et al.*, 2002, pp.671, 678).

The UK, on the other hand, exemplifies a state which is actively exclusive in that it seeks to prevent the formation and activities of social movements that oppose its agenda. It is a tendency strongest in states with a market liberal ideology which interpret the motives of autonomous social groups in terms of materialism and self-interest. The interests of such groups are therefore seen to be socially costly and destructive of economic efficiency – and thus to be undermined and opposed by all legitimate means as state operations became more centralized and secretive. This tendency was strongest during the Thatcher years, 1979–90, leading the UK into the position of being 'the only European outpost of radical market liberalism, with an authoritarian, actively exclusive state to match'. It was not just the UK *state* that showed such exceptional characteristics – British environmentalists were not very participatory or democratic in practice either and their numerous representatives had done little to develop much in the way of a social movement (Dryzek *et al.*, 2002, pp.661, 676).

This comparative analysis presents only one perspective on contemporary state forms, and focuses in a relatively specialized manner on those whose regime is liberal democratic in character and which emerge directly from the European state tradition. Examination of this kind of state, where cases are already similar in nature, enables a finer-grain analysis which uncovers differences that are quite specific in character. It also presents a sharper perspective on the nature of the contemporary state and the influence it exerts on political outcomes.

A political regime – such as that of liberal democracy, which is established in the countries examined here (Germany, Norway, the UK and the USA) – is not the same thing as the state itself or the institutional apparatus it embodies, although the links between the two are strong, both in empirical and conceptual terms. What this analysis shows, though, is that the structure of the state itself and the way it operates has a strong influence on the practice of liberal democracy and the political outcomes it produces in a particular country; in this case: whether favourable conditions exist for the development of social movements such as those of the environmentalists; and how far they are able to articulate their interests, impact on the policy process and influence government decisions. In short – and to return to the beginning of this chapter and the issue of how far the state is now in question – the state *is* significant and its structures *do have* a distinct impact on political outcomes. The state is by no means universally superseded and how it operates can have important political consequences.

SUMMARY

- Alongside the increasingly predominant democratic state there are also various other contemporary forms.
- Significant differences can be identified between the contemporary forms of capitalist democratic state.
- These suggest that the state still exercises a decisive influence on political outcomes in the established democracies.

THE ROLE OF THE CONTEMPORARY STATE

In recent decades certain factors have led analysts to question whether we might be starting to witness the decline of the nation-state. Indeed, some have gone so far as to speak of 'the death of the nation-state'. A simple version of the argument is that the role of the state is placed in question because its power, effectiveness and sovereignty are being eroded from above and below.

It has lost its former centrality and been challenged by its own peripheries, and it has itself been peripheralized by an increasingly interconnected global system. In terms of the threat from above the state is, first, increasingly constrained and under pressure from the dynamics of the world economy. States are pressed by their populations to exercise what control they can, attract inward investment and mitigate this insecurity.

This has two major consequences. In domestic policy, Gourevitch (1986, p.33) has argued that most governments have been pressed in the same direction: to reduce state spending and intervention as measures to achieve full employment, because these would reduce the state's competitive edge in global markets. There is, equally, a clear trend among states at all levels to subordinate social policy to the 'needs' of labour market flexibility and structural competitiveness; that is, social expenditure should be reduced where it is not directly related to enhanced flexibility and competitiveness in the use of capital resources. The trend also involves attempts to roll back the state and reduce the welfare rights that were established under the post-war class compromises.

Externally, the important consequence of such developments is that global forces mean that states must cooperate more intensively at the regional or global level. This is illustrated by the growth of regional institutions such as the EU, as well as the influence of global institutions such as the International Monetary Fund (a UN agency established to expand international trade and encourage economic development) and the Group of Seven (an association of the seven countries with the biggest economies) which exercise powerful functions of economic coordination.

A second source of the threat from above comes from the weak capacity of the state to cope with the rapidly widening range of transnational problems. The result is:

> a significant shift towards multilateral diplomacy and collective action [and] a staggering increase in the number of inter-governmental organizations and international regimes ... Most western governments are so deeply enmeshed in these regulatory and decision-making structures that national and international

policy making have become inseparable. In effect, the 'internationalisation' of the state has created forms of international governance in which collective policy making and coordination of policy between governments have become vital to the achievement of national and international goals.

(McGrew, 1992b, pp.88–9)

State bureaucracies themselves become internationalized, making it difficult for ministers and governments to retain direct control. This process of internationalization is widely held to have broadened yet weakened the national state.

We can say, therefore, that the forces of globalization have begun to dissolve the form and weaken the autonomy of the advanced capitalist state as it cedes a measure of control and authority to suprastate bodies. By doing so, it progressively loses the role it once played. This in turn can affect legitimacy: no government gains popularity by explaining to its population that its hands are tied by the constraints of the global market. One familiar characterization of this, for example in relation to the UK and the EU, is to say that in this process the state's absolute autonomy and sovereignty have been eroded.

However, it is also possible to argue against this. If sovereign states actively shape, or voluntarily agree to be bound by, new international 'regimes', then they are 'the determinants as well as the objects of an expanding field of regulatory practices'. In some areas, sovereignty is clearly divided or limited by participation in these regimes, but in others the effectiveness of the state may be enhanced (McGrew, 1992a, p.109). This indicates that the case for decreasing autonomy is not clear-cut, or at least needs to be made with reservations.

We now turn to consider threats 'from below'. In the more advanced capitalist states, a clear process of fragmentation appears to be taking place. We wrote earlier about the 'state sponsored' nationalism, which powerfully affected the birth and consolidation of most modern nation-states. It is hard to deny that for a very long time, and along many dimensions, it has been successful. For example, in the case of the UK, there are many different ethnic and religious groups, yet it is reasonable to assume that most people do feel British to some degree, and take some pride in the nation's history and cultural heritage. One might further argue that the nation has in the past 'pulled together' with impressive unity in war and that, having contributed to defeating fascism in the Second World War, British liberal democracy has presided over more than 50 years of relative peace and rising prosperity for the British as a whole. The level of opposition to British participation in the invasion of Iraq in 2003 was therefore that much more striking.

There are now clear signs that this identity, as part of a particular cultural fabric, is beginning to unravel and that the suppression of local and particular cultures by those who directed the centralized and centralizing nation-state was never entirely successful or complete. Such 'local nationalism' now often sees a more attractive opportunity in associations, such as the EU, which are beyond the traditional state. In the British context, Stuart Hall has expressed this drive for self-expression and self-advancement as 'attempting to bypass blockages of various kinds at the national level – Scotland's dream of breaking the English connection and restoring its Enlightenment links with Europe; the possibility of subsuming Northern Ireland's intractable problems in some sort of European solution' (Hall, 1999, p.37).

We have a seeming paradox in contemporary nationalism. State nationalism begins to fragment as unity, effectiveness and legitimacy decline. At the same time the smaller, local nationalisms gain focus and momentum as they became more confident. This phenomenon has been described as 'the confusing spectacle of what we might call ascending and descending nationalisms' (Hall, 1999, p.37). It is germane for our purposes, however, that the ambition of most of these local nationalisms is generally still couched in terms of establishing their own state, that the vehicle in which these groups wish to pursue their own destiny is still seen in that familiar shape. In the case of the East European nations, it may be that they feel nationhood in state form is the only passport that will give them access to the prosperity of Western Europe.

It may well be possible that we are feeling our way towards what has been called 'a changing architecture' for the modern state. The taken-for-granted *national* focus of political organization and action is being displaced by a marked dispersion of politics and policy issues to other scales or levels of activity. A process of 'de-nationalization' has been identified: that is, not only does the state transfer power to supranational bodies, but it also delegates authority to subordinate levels of territorial organization. One feature of this may be a move towards decentralization or devolution **(Guibernau, 2005)**; an equally significant feature is a shift from government to *governance* on various territorial scales and across various functional domains **(Charlesworth and Humphreys, 2005)**. There is less exercise of power from formal political centres such as the state, and more diffuse processes of accommodation and negotiation on an international scale with diverse sources of influence and power. Thus there has been a 'rescaling' of the state, and a broad reorganization of the state and the critical processes of contemporary politics (Jessop, 2002, pp.177–201).

In this view the national state is far from being functionally redundant. It continues to exercise a crucial coordinating and regulating function over the array of new bodies in public–private initiatives of all kinds. One simple example is the privatization of the public utilities in the UK. Industries and services such as those providing gas, electricity, the telephone service or railways may no longer be run by the state, but they are most certainly coordinated by complex legislation and regulated by official scrutiny through public agencies.

So the charge of erosion and decline is at least partially countered by such change and renewal in the state's form and mode of operation. In the domestic sphere, Jessop (2002, p.199) also points out, the 'resort to governance' can enhance the state's capacity to project its influence and secure its objectives by mobilizing knowledge and power resources from influential non-governmental partners or stakeholders. By participating in international bodies, states can in some respects increase their effectiveness, that is, get more of what they want.

SUMMARY

- States are increasingly under pressure from the dynamics of the world economy, which restrains their freedom to act in domestic social policy.
- The widening range of transnational problems also diminishes the state's capacity for independent action.
- Processes of internal fragmentation weaken the state as an established entity, but often strengthen the ideal of statehood for groups aspiring to a collective identity.
- The changing architecture of the state involves various trends and counter trends in the process of state restructuring.

8 CONCLUSION

We began this chapter by suggesting that the state is in question, by processes essentially located above the central state and others rooted in activities and institutions below state level or on the periphery of existing political systems. We then defined the terms with which we can analyse the state, trace the evolution of the modern state historically, and observe the processes of centralization and cultural homogenization that have produced the distinctive and powerful form of the state as we now encounter it. In the West some nations went through that process two centuries ago, others have not progressed as far along that road.

At the turn of the twenty-first century, there is some evidence of the process going into reverse, at least for those older nation-states, as the authority of the centre is challenged anew from the periphery. At the same time, elements of political and economic globalization are producing changes in the form and functioning of the state. From this perspective we have looked at both the state's internationalization, and at what has been called the de-nationalization of the state's relation with civil society. The state is in this sense 'in question' in ways that were not detected a few decades ago.

In some respects the state is being pushed to the periphery itself. How far the autonomy and effectiveness of the modern state are being affected by these developments has been examined as an open question and there are clearly arguments on both sides. We have touched on just a little of the enormous volume of literature on the theory and practice of the state and a range of the questions that have been posed. This should be sufficient for you to have some idea of how far and why the contemporary state is now in question.

REFERENCES

Bobbio, N. (1987) *The Future of Democracy*, Cambridge, Polity Press.

Charlesworth, J. and Humphreys, W.D. (2005) 'Challenging centre–periphery relations in health policy' in Prokhovnik, R. (ed.) *Making Policy, Shaping Lives*, Edinburgh, Edinburgh University Press/The Open University.

Cox, R. (1997) 'Democracy in hard times: economic globalization and the limits to liberal democracy' in McGrew, A. (ed.) *The Transformation of Democracy*, Cambridge, Polity Press.

Dryzek, J., Hunold, C. and Schlosberg, D. with Downs, D. and Hernes, H.-K. (2002) 'Environmental transformation of the state: the USA, Norway, Germany and the UK', *Political Studies*, vol.50, no.4, pp.659–82.

Guibernau, M. (2005) 'Centre–periphery relations: government beyond Westminister' in Hefferman, R. and Thompson, G.F. (eds) *Politics and Power in the UK*, Edinburgh, Edinburgh University Press/The Open University.

Gill, G. (2003) *The Nature and Development of the Modern State*, Houndmills, Palgrave Macmillan.

Gourevitch, P.A. (1986) *Politics in Hard Times: Comparative Responses to International Economic Crises*, New York, Cornell University Press.

Hall, S. (1999) 'Culture, community and nation' in Boswell, D. and Evans, J. (eds) *Representing the Nation*, London, Routledge.

Held, D. (1992) 'The development of the modern state' in Hall, S. and Gieben, B. (eds) *Formations of Modernity*, Cambridge, Polity Press.

Jessop, B. (2002) *The Future of the Capitalist State*, Cambridge, Polity.

Karatnycky, A. (ed.) (2001) *Freedom in the World: Annual Survey of Political Rights and Civil Liberties*, New York, Freedom House.

Mann, M. (1988) *The Sources of Social Power Volume 1: A History of Power from the Beginning to AD 1760*, Cambridge, Cambridge University Press.

Mann, M. (1993) *The Sources of Social Power Volume 2: The Rise of Classes and Nation-States, 1760–1914*, Cambridge, Cambridge University Press.

McGrew, A. (1992a) 'The state: advanced capitalist societies' in Allan, J., Braham, P. and Lewis, P.G. (eds) *Political and Economic Forms of Modernity*, Cambridge, Polity.

McGrew, A. (1992b) 'A global society' in Hall, S., Held, D. and McGrew, A. (eds) *Modernity and its Futures*, Cambridge, Polity.

Poggi, G. (1978) *The Development of the Modern State*, London, Hutchison.

Weber, M. (1964) *The Theory of Social and Economic Organization*, trans. Henderson, A. and Parsons, T. (eds), New York, Free Press.

FURTHER READING

Gill, G. (2003) *The Nature and Development of the Modern State*, Houndmills, Palgrave Macmillan.

Hall, S. and Gieben, B. (eds) (1992) *Formations of Modernity*, Cambridge, Polity Press.

Poggi, G. (1978) *The Development of the Modern State*, London, Hutchison.

Taking part in politics

Mark J. Smith

Contents

1 INTRODUCTION

Liberal democracies are often associated with free and fair elections and open scrutiny of legislation and policies. Yet at the same time there is much discussion of growing disillusionment and civic apathy towards the decisions and actions of governments (Chapter 1). As a result, it is important to think about the following questions.

- Is political participation on the slide or are new forms of engagement taking the place of voting and joining political parties?

- Do we need to examine the political issues in everyday life as much as the big issues of the day in order to understand the motives for participation?

- How effective are the different electoral systems in channelling participation and ensuring that citizens have their views represented?

- Do pressure groups and social movements provide an alternative mechanism to political parties for mediating participation and dissent?

When considering these questions, this chapter compares and contrasts different kinds of political systems. To start addressing these questions, we need to specify what *participation* means. Although we will examine *dissent* more specifically later in the chapter, we need to acknowledge that it is not easy to separate participation and dissent. If a citizen engages in a sit-down demonstration on a highway or other form of non-violent civil disobedience in opposition to a government policy, this does not preclude them from writing to their elected representative or being engaged in fund-raising for a pressure group. Indeed, it is possible to participate through the conventional political processes on some issues but dissent on others. So, participation and dissent are closely related. For the time being let's accept that participation involves citizens assenting to or dissenting from the policies and decisions of political leaders and the social values they represent.

Dissenters – so called because of their historical rejection of the doctrines of dominant religious beliefs – express opinions which lie outside the normal boundaries of debate on an issue or principle. Since social values and norms change, the views expressed by dissenters in one place and time may *become the norm* against which dissent is raised in another. Some forms of dissent, however, cannot strictly be considered as forms of participation because they challenge the political system itself in ways that are considered to be illegitimate, such as through acts of terrorism.

When we consider participation in politics, we are looking at how citizens are involved (or not) in the decisions that affect their lives. Participation is often associated with citizens responding either critically or affirmatively to new legislation and changes in government funding for public services such as health care and education. In these cases, participation is mediated through elected representatives or organized groups. In other situations, citizens lobby directly the national, regional or local assembly or join a demonstration.

This chapter starts by considering the role of participation (and non-participation) in our understanding of democratic politics, before moving on to examine how political parties and electoral systems organize our political actions. Sometimes these party and electoral systems have positive outcomes, but they can also lead to crisis and instability. While comparison is useful, it is important not to lose sight of the very different political contexts in each society. The chapter also argues that we should take into account how participation can take place in a variety of ways and contexts beyond that of voting and active membership.

2   DEMOCRACY AND PARTICIPATION: VOTING AND NON-VOTING

Democracies are viewed as political systems where, in some sense, power is held by all of the people (Chapter 2). But what does this mean in practice when adults of voting age exceed 40 million, as in the UK or France? With that number of people, the opportunity for many to have a real impact in making political decisions is almost negligible. For most people that just leaves the minimal participation of voting. Even there, in the 2001 general election in the UK, for example, two out of every five eligible voters did not even cast a vote.

It is difficult to imagine how all citizens of a nation-state can participate directly in national government. Once a political community exceeds, say, ten thousand citizens, there are real limits on effective direct participation for individuals and smaller groups. In light of this, we can say that the best alternative system involves electors voting for candidates to act on their behalf (regardless of whether individual electors voted for the winning candidate or not). Of course, this means that political representatives are faced with the competing, and possibly incompatible, demands of many electors.

In representative democracies, elected representatives are ideally seen, not as mouthpieces for special and sectarian interests, but as legislators acting on behalf of the collective, public or national interest (as defined by the representative's conscience). Thus, the principle of representation is regarded as important both as an effective surrogate for direct participation and as a channel for political participation. In most cases, elections involve choices between parties rather than between the virtues of different candidates and, in Western European societies, loyalty towards political parties as the prime institutions of democracy has been significant for over a century.

Depending on your view, democratic institutions can be seen as enabling or constraining participation. You could argue that the election of representatives is a practical solution to ensuring some forms of participation in a manageable way. Alternatively, you could argue that much depends on the quality of the institutional mechanisms for responding to the concerns of citizens in representative democracies. There is no easy answer to this but most political systems try to strike a balance between the representation of diverse interests and the formation of an effective legislature and government.

It might still be reasonable to claim that an actively involved citizenry would be an essential prerequisite for an effective democratic process. Political scientists differ in their views on this. Advocates of active participation, such as the American philosopher John Dewey, believe that a well-educated population will create a context within which debate can be thorough and political decisions made that really do address the needs and wants of citizens. An alternative approach argues that widespread participation in politics is a response to crises in political representation and is also usually symptomatic of wider socio-economic conflict. According to this view, widespread apathy can actually be taken as an expression of satisfaction with the political system and the decisions made by elites rather than as an expression of alienation and disillusion.

Some comparative studies of democratization have suggested that stable democracies have witnessed the construction of political institutions first, followed later by mass politics. For example, Robert Dahl (1971, 1989) states that the most effective democratic systems arise as a result of the evolution of a process of contestation between exclusive and elite political factions, later becoming political parties, long before the slow steps to greater inclusivity (in the steps towards universal suffrage). In this way, factions, parties and orderly competition between them became deeply embedded in the conduct of both the state and civil society well before all social groups participated in elections. The rules of the political game facilitated contestation within elites and then, when civility and mutual trust were established, the system was robust enough to cope with a more inclusive politics. Dahl suggests that this road to democratization was one followed in England and Sweden, whereas in the German case, prior to the Nazi regime, inclusivity preceded contestation, resulting in a party system that was fragile and unable to deal with the competing forces involved.

According to Dahl (1971, 1989) democracies are weaker when legitimacy has not been established and when the political institutions for conflict resolution are undeveloped. In this account, the onus seems to be on mainstream political parties and the legislative assemblies to constitute the stabilizing forces. Yet, if this is the case, how do we explain the growth and proliferation of social movements that operate independently or loosely attached to mainstream political parties in Western societies? Whether Dahl is right or wrong on how parties affect democratic political systems, his stress on the important role played by the cultural context of politics is an essential starting point. The cultural location of each citizen can have a profound effect on their motives for political participation (see Box 3.1) and the reasons for political participation are complex. Factors such as the weather can affect whether people turn out to vote – a poor turn-out due to bad weather was traditionally thought to disadvantage left-wing parties.

BOX 3.1   **What drives citizens to participate in party politics?**

Habit and cultural homogeneity
In stable, close-knit and often insular communities, voting support for particular parties tends to be solid over long periods of time with support for specific political parties or movements becoming customary; party affiliation becomes part of the way we define ourselves. With greater social and geographical mobility in Western societies since the Second World War, this kind of strong identification is less widespread.

Socialization
Loyalty to political affiliations can be deeply embedded in families and communities.

Ideological conviction
This involves sharing a vision of the society that should be constructed or enabled to evolve.

Pragmatic goal seeking
Some electors participate in an instrumental way based on rational or instrumental calculations concerned, for example, with public services or tax cuts. In some cases, these electors become involved with local constituencies because it facilitates personal advancement.

Charismatic leadership
Certain political leaders have been able to generate an emotional response and build populist alliances across social groups in unusual ways, appealing to individuals above the heads of their traditional political ties (such as Margaret Thatcher's appeal to skilled trade unionists in Britain).

Knee-jerk politics
This means responding to a perceived problem such as urban decay and social marginalization by supporting a political party which offers a supposedly easy solution (for example, the National Front in France and the British National Party, which promise an end to immigration as a panacea for the social exclusion and material deprivation of the white working class).

If we take voter turn-out as an index of participation, liberal democracies from France to Finland and from the UK to the USA seem to be suffering from a decline in civic commitment. In many Western political systems, voter turn-out has steadily declined over the late twentieth century (although in some countries, for example Australia, voting remains compulsory). Average turn-out in Western Europe during each post-war decade ranged from 81.7 to 84.9 per cent until the 1990s, when it fell to 77.6 per cent. Of course, voting turn-out has increased due to intense national debates, such as in Norway in 1997, the UK in 1992, the USA in 2000, and in some Eastern European elections as post-communist democracies have consolidated.

A crucial question currently being investigated by political researchers is whether there is an increasing sense of apathy towards political decisions. Is voting viewed – perhaps correctly – as an ineffective way of influencing politics, the product of disillusion of specific groups of people, such as younger voters? Is political participation taking different forms? The rise of non-voting involves a combination of these factors. While the decline in voter turn-out has been empirically demonstrated, this decline has been of a smaller level than is often assumed. According to Franklin (2004), most Western societies have witnessed a variation of 5 per cent from the mean average in the years 1945–99. More interesting for the future of participation, is the lower level of voting by younger age groups. Franklin argues that voting is habitual and that particular age groups maintain a fairly consistent level of turn-out during their lifetimes. If younger cohorts of voters continue to have a lower level of turn-out, then the overall turn-out will decline over the next 30 years as the electorate changes. However, this will depend on whether this level of turn-out is sustained by successive cohorts of younger voters. Small changes now may herald a larger decline in this kind of political participation in future.

When interpreting statistical evidence (such as that shown in Table 3.1) we should also note that 5–15 per cent of the electorate don't vote due to administrative factors (electoral registers are always out of date when published) and local authority tax evasion, as well as for other reasons, such as ill-health, disability, accident or because they do not know about postal or proxy voting. In addition, many constituencies only have a limited range of candidates and some supporters of the smaller political parties cannot bring themselves to vote for another party, as is the case for many supporters of the Green Party who may not vote at all when there is no Green candidate. The uncommitted, disillusioned or plain overworked still play a part, but there is no certainty on the balance between non-voting by the disaffected and non-voting by those who wish to make an anti-parliamentary point.

TABLE 3.1   Turn-out for the UK General Election, 2001

Country	Electorate	Total vote	Turn-out (%)
England	36,990,780	21,870,488	59.12
Northern Ireland	1,191,009	810,381	68.04
Scotland	3,983,306	2,313,581	58.08
Wales	2,236,143	1,372,542	61.38

Source: The Electoral Commission, 2002

SUMMARY

- Representative democracy provides a mechanism for reconciling the diverse opinions and interests of citizens, so that agreement can be reached on the direction of society in a way that citizens consider to be legitimate.

- Apathy is an emerging feature of politics among younger cohorts of citizens and, if non-voting remains habitual in each new cohort, as each generation of voters ages then voter turn-out could fall dramatically in the future.

- The motives for participation are complex and varied, so understanding how individuals become involved demands close attention to the cultural context of citizens.

3 IS THE PARTY OVER? PARTICIPATION IN THE INSTITUTIONAL CONTEXT

Political parties serve to organize citizens with more or less compatible goals in order to represent their views, values, interests and, sometimes, prejudices. As agencies of participation, parties usually have to find a way of balancing the need to maintain their core support at the same time as making themselves attractive to segments of society that do not strongly identify with the party's core values. As such, parties provide horizontal linkages between different kinds of groups and vertical linkages that serve to encourage communication between the political arena and citizens. The reconciliation of divergent interests achieved through parties provides a vital integrative function in democratic political systems.

The existence of competing parties vying for support ensures that electors have choice in elections and hence that governing parties can be held accountable:

a party can lose power if it fails to secure the consent of a significant part of the voting electorate. Parties also act as recruitment mechanisms for grooming politicians and, if successful in elections, provide the personnel for filling positions in government from the local through to the national levels.

While party politics is an essential underpinning to Western democratic institutions, party membership is in decline in many democratic political systems. If citizens are participating in non-party ways, this raises questions about how parliamentary and governmental bodies can draw on their talents. How can we explain the fall in party membership? First, we need to address the reasons for becoming a party member. Political parties should be seen as social circles as much as having purely political goals. The social functions of bringing people together with similar values and social backgrounds serve as a motivator for membership just as much as having strong convictions on a particular issue. This applies across the political spectrum and to both national and regional parties. For example, the Party for Independent Normandy and the Scottish National Party provide arenas for sustaining minority identities, and Abertzaleen Batasuna (the Basque nationalist coalition) and Plaid Cymru for defending linguistic and cultural heritages.

On the right-wing, party members tend to be drawn from business and professional backgrounds though there is also a marked tendency for many members to be older and to be committed to the traditional social hierarchy as well as to law-and-order politics. Green and socialist parties tend to bring together people with strong commitment to radical social change and, often with this, a commitment to adopting an unconventional lifestyle. (See Figure 3.1.)

FIGURE 3.1   Political party archetypes

Having a largely homogeneous social composition can provide a party with a clear sense of purpose. However, while such members are in their different ways anti-establishment, these 'different ways' can make for deep divisions on what the focus of political activity should be. Even in parties with a long history of cohesion there can be significant shifts in values that cause significant problems for sustaining the support of members. In European societies, the movement of right-wing parties towards free market policies and the assertion of economic individualism have generated problems of commitment for members with a traditional commitment to order and responsibility.

It is important to recognize that participation has, until recently, been largely expressed and channelled through political parties or through movements closely affiliated with political parties. This is no longer the case in many Western European societies where a combination of disillusionment with mainstream political parties and the opening up of new opportunities for participation on single issues has changed the landscape. A key question is whether this is a result of a broader trend or something quite specific to Western Europe.

This is where comparative analysis is especially useful. We find that the picture is slightly different in Eastern Europe where, until the 1990s, political parties were generally associated with authoritarian rule and operated as a mechanism of integration in a complex system of patronage or preferment. Membership of the dominant single parties of communist societies was the key route for social mobility, and the resources of the state (such as health services and housing) were distributed in a preferential way to party members. In addition, alternative political organizations had been ruthlessly suppressed by state security organizations or by military force, as in Hungary (1956), in Czechoslovakia (1968) and in the case of the trade union Solidarity in Poland (1981). In short, when constructing a democratic political system, political parties were seen as part of the problem rather than the solution and this was reflected in the political movements that mobilized against the communist regimes throughout Eastern Europe (see Box 3.2 overleaf).

For Lewis (2001), the factors at play are in part a product of the historically and culturally specific experiences of communist control. Indeed, although the idea of liberal multi-party systems is seen as a better alternative, the historical experience of party politics in Eastern Europe indicates that relatively low party membership and electoral turn-outs are to be expected. Lewis draws a distinction between transition phases (as illustrated in Figure 3.2) and democratic consolidation where political parties play a more active role, especially in managing conflict and constructing national political communities. Here, he identifies different pathways in the Eastern European experience. The experiences of the Czech Republic, Hungary and Slovenia provide evidence of stable party systems running the course of a full constitutional term, sufficiently robust to manage the ethnic tensions that had

BOX 3.2   **Political parties in emerging Eastern European democracies**

Political parties were ... not prominent in the early stages of democratic transition in post-communist Europe. The leading players were broad social movements and unified national fronts rather than individually constituted political parties. Solidarity in Poland and Civic Forum/Public Against Violence in Czechoslovakia, Sajudis in Lithuania and Popular Fronts in Latvia and Estonia, a Union of Democratic Forces in Bulgaria and National Salvation Front in Romania – the latter an anomalous political force in that it cloaked reform communists and those associated with the former regime rather than forces of national and anti-communist opposition.

Nearly all of these formations (the exception was Bulgaria) won freely contested elections or major political victories in 1990 (1989 in the case of Poland), as did the Croatian Democratic Union and the DEMOS popular coalition in Slovenia. The Popular Front of Moldova was also victorious, although communist forces prevailed in the other post-Soviet states of Belarus and Ukraine (as they did in slightly different guise in Serbia and Montenegro). A Democratic Party was dominant amongst opposition forces during the slow unfreezing of Albanian political life, but it soon lost to regrouped communist forces in the election of March 1991.

Only in Hungary was the initial election fought by organizations that looked like autonomous parties, and even here the victor went under the title of Hungarian Democratic Forum. Parties, however, soon began to emerge within the broad fronts although the formation of anything like viable organizations and stable party systems was a problematic process. The Bulgarian Union of Democratic Forces and Romanian National Salvation Front retained a core political identity but also underwent a process of fragmentation. In general, the unity of the social movements soon dissipated, although a successful electoral coalition was reformed in Poland on the basis of the Solidarity trade union and won through to form a government in 1997.

Even in the countries further along the path of democratic development, the parties that were formed and which henceforth prevailed in the political scene tended to be informally organized, elitist and dominated by a narrow coterie of leaders ... The transformation of opposition movements into democratic parties can indeed be seen as a critical moment in the democratization process, and one that opens the way to the consolidation of new regimes rather than their being caught in some halfway house of transitional change or regression back to authoritarian rule. The support of a reasonably well developed civil society and the opportunities it offers for the development of institutions like parties, labour unions and interest associations have been of great importance for the outcome of different processes of democratization (Gill, 2000: 240–1). It provides conditions for the transformation of loosely organized, ideologically diffuse movements into more structured, goal-oriented bodies that have the capacity to operate within an ordered political system.

(Lewis, 2001, pp.546, 550)

been suppressed under communism and, in the case of the Czech Republic, a corruption scandal in 1997.

FIGURE 3.2   Strength through unity: Lech Walesa and other members of a Solidarnosc demonstration, Cracow, Poland

Lewis notes how the new post-communist party system in Czechoslovakia gave voice to serious ethnic rivalries, while at the same time provided an institutional mechanism for peacefully and constitutionally splitting the country into two. More problematic cases of democratic consolidation can be seen in Slovakia, Bulgaria and Macedonia, where party systems have so far failed to provide the necessary forms of social integration. These are cases where there are problems in constructing a viable political community and where there are ethnic conflicts, difficulties in separating the political and economic control, territorial disagreements (as in the former Yugoslavia) and where political leaders display intolerance to opposition and a tendency to return to the tried and tested authoritarian techniques of the previous regimes.

Moreover, success stories have often been associated with the absence of such difficulties. Political parties are not usually the first port of call for active citizens and (other than in Austria and the Scandinavian societies) only about 1–5 per cent of electors are actively engaged in party activities (Mair and van Biezen, 2001). In addition, transnational television and other electronic media mean that political parties no longer offer the same opportunities for social integration, nor are they capable of mobilizing the population in the manner of political parties in the early twentieth century. As in Western Europe, the distinction between political parties and interest groups or new social movements is not clear-cut and a more appropriate starting point is to look for looser configurations of parties and non-party groups.

SUMMARY

- In most European societies, when citizens feel driven to participate in politics, other than the seismic drive to topple an authoritarian regime, it is largely a response to a specific issue, a defence of their own material interests or in order to promote a cause.

- Between election campaigns, political participation is often channelled through a wide range of pressure groups which attempt to make demands on the political system and provide a check on the activities of governments.

- Comparing the operation of parties (or groups) as mechanisms for participation enables us to identify the conditions for stable democratic systems, while recognizing the cultural differences in each case.

4 AUDITING PARTICIPATION: WIDENING THE NET

This chapter started by highlighting the possibility that the decline in voting rates and political party membership levels could be a result of declining trust in the institutions and personnel in public life. Recent research has shed light on these factors. The Citizen Audit conducted by Seyd, Whiteley and Pattie involved a random sample (of 24,000 individuals, eliciting over 13,000 responses) drawn from England, Scotland and Wales with the purpose of comparing participation across different regions and to take account of the effects of devolution in Scotland and Wales (Seyd *et al.*, 2001, pp.141–8). (Few studies produce responses on such a massive scale: there were 9959 responses from the 21,000 mail questionnaires, and 3457 individuals were interviewed by the team.) This study of democracy and participation explores the different dimensions of trust in political processes but casts a wide net when considering the kinds of activities that can be considered to be a feature of political participation. In addition, it is as much concerned with attitudes as with participative actions in order to understand the who, why and how of participation. To help make sense of the complex empirical evidence, Seyd *et al.* use ideal types (simplistic but useful exaggerations such as orthodox/unorthodox forms of participation, formal/ informal activities, group/individual behaviour and actual/potential participation). In this section we look at some of the detail of what the Citizen Audit revealed.

Let's start with the question of *how* people participate. People can belong to, participate in or donate money to political organizations. In terms of orthodox participation, there are various campaigning organizations which represent occupational, religious, cultural and recreational groups that have a national presence. Individually, the focus has often been on voting, on signing petitions or on citizens contacting politicians and public officials through activities such as lobbying or writing letters. On the unorthodox side of participation, there are local and voluntary networks which provide support for specific groups (such as meals-on-wheels or victim support groups), group activities (such as industrial action), and individual participation in the form of contact with providers of local and regional services (for example, parents contacting the school governors or the head teacher, and patients complaining to hospital administrators). Indeed, being a school governor is as valid for understanding the processes through which political decisions are made as being a local councillor or Member of the European Parliament.

To understand political participation, then, we need a conception of the political that focuses on the everyday activities of citizens. In particular, we need to take account of the fact that people feel they have an obligation to get involved as well as to engage in defending and exercising their rights. Rights and obligations are closely related.

The Citizen Audit has revealed that, despite the fact that most individuals hold politicians in low regard, that fewer people strongly identify with a specific political party than in the past and that voting rates are on the decline, this does not mean that people are disengaged. Participation may still be a minority sport, nevertheless it involves large numbers of people. By defining political activity more broadly to take account of everyday citizenship, there is substantial evidence of engagement with political processes. The Citizen Audit identifies two extensive forms of participation: membership and cheque book participation.

- *Membership*
  Approximately 40 per cent of adults (19 million) belong to at least one political organization ranging from trade unions and environmental campaigning groups to neighbourhood or community groups (with half this number belonging to more than one). For example, 2.5 million belong to residential organizations and 1.75 million to conservation groups. This joining has a qualitative dimension for most joiners of sports clubs, consumer groups, church circles and PTAs; there are, though, some exceptions – for instance, most join the National Trust to acquire concessionary rates for tourist activities.

- *Cheque book participation*
  Providing financial support for activists is also widespread, and high for organizations concerned with the rights of patients (37 per cent), people with disabilities (32 per cent), ex-service personnel (23 per cent) and for protecting animals (25 per cent).

The finding that 62 per cent make donations may be interpreted as an indication that many advocate the rights of specific people or animals. However, we have to tread carefully. It would be stretching a point to suggest that because 25 per cent donated money to an organization concerned with animals, this amounted to a quarter of these citizens believing in animal rights (it is more likely that they are motivated by a concern for animal welfare). Some donations may result from the desire to develop new medical treatments or provide respite care for the parents of disabled children or food for animal rescue centres. Such donations are an indication of values, but the key question is which values? There is also evidence of participation through activities such as signing petitions (42 per cent) or wearing badges and stickers (21 per cent).

More conventional kinds of political participation such as contacting officials and becoming involved in group activities, including protests, were less frequently mentioned in the audit (they demand considerable time and energy). Only 5 per cent of those surveyed indicated they had participated in a demonstration, but this research was conducted before the largest demonstrations in the history of the UK (the 'liberty and livelihood' march in 2002, and the 'Stop the Iraq war' march in 2003). However, demonstrations, vigils and other direct action protests remain highly visible forms of participation that still enable the more dedicated citizenry to have an impact.

In the following sections, we turn to the social bases of participation and how political behaviour is changing, to see how established patterns of political choices can generate different results depending on the institutional context.

SUMMARY

- The Citizen Audit study suggests that we need to consider a broader repertoire of activities of political participation.
- There is little evidence of widespread apathy and/or satisfaction with the way in which politics is conducted: most citizens focus their participation in ways that are more likely to achieve their objectives or which respond directly to the issues that most concern them.

5 MEDIATING POLITICS: IDENTITIES, PARTIES AND ELECTORAL SYSTEMS

Consider what has changed in the way people assume political identifications. Political researchers have often sought explanations of political behaviour by referring to the social position of individuals. Voting patterns have often been explained by reference to social cleavages such as class location (with the working class defined occupationally in terms of manual work). In this way the bedrock of the support for the Socialist and Communist Parties in France, the Social Democrats in Germany and the Labour Party in the UK was achieved through close links with the labour movement. Political scientists were so struck with the normality of social class location as a motivator for voting that middle-class citizens voting for left-wing parties and working-class citizens voting for right-wing parties were characterized as examples of 'deviant voting'.

Of course, the actual picture was much more complicated than this. Nevertheless, broad patterns could be identified, such as the effect of parental socialization, the higher propensity of women to vote for centre-right parties, the role of political generations (such as the generation radicalized by the experiences of the Depression and of war in Europe) and the impact of neighbourhood or locality effects. In each case it was assumed that social behaviour was shaped by social structures. For example, right-wing and conservative politicians constructed their policies as being concerned more with family life and the domestic sphere together with emphasizing the importance of religious values (at a time when women were more likely than men to actively participate in religious practices).

Since the 1950s, Western societies have experienced substantial social change. In particular, general levels of education are higher and individuals are more geographically and socially mobile. Occupational change has meant that manual labour is now a minority in the workforce, while many non-manual occupations do not carry high status and rewards. Families, neighbourhoods, communities and traditional collective movements, such as trade unions, no longer offer useful predictors of voting behaviour or party membership. Citizens are more instrumental and policy oriented. In addition, older citizens identify more strongly with a particular political party than younger people do. Thus, over time, as a product of demographic change, an electorate aligned with specific parties is giving way to an electorate made up of more highly educated citizens who are weak identifiers – well informed about politics but less likely to have strong convictions. To see how this has affected political systems, it is useful to compare two societies with quite different electoral systems, those of the UK and Germany.

Unlike most other European societies, British national elections adopt the single member plurality system (SMPS), often referred to as 'first past the post' (or FPTP). Here, the candidate with the largest number of votes in each constituency wins the seat. In this way, with the exception of short periods in the 1970s and briefly in the mid 1990s, one political party secured a majority in the key legislative chamber, the House of Commons. The volatility of voting support in the context of SMPS has produced some unexpected results in terms of representation of political parties in the British parliament. Even small surges of support in just a limited number of seats have ensured that the winning party has enjoyed a majority in excess of 100 seats in four of the last six elections. In 2001, when the Conservatives and Liberal Democrats both received below 30 per cent of the vote, New Labour won 412 seats with only 40.7 per cent of the vote (compared with the combined total of 246 seats for all opposing parties). In short, the winning party is likely to achieve a 'landslide victory', not as a result of popular support but through the division of the electorate by opposing political parties. At no point has a majority of the seats corresponded to a majority vote, though the virtue of SMPS is that it produces clear-cut electoral decisions with single-party governments able to exercise leadership.

In the British case the party which comes third in terms of the number of votes and achieves second place in the majority of seats, suffers from under-representation in the parliament. In European political systems which have proportional representation (PR), the smaller parties have a much more influential role. Casting a vote is one thing, but then there is a burning question of whether it counts. In some electoral systems, such as those in Israel and Sweden, seats in the legislative chamber are allocated in direct proportion to the votes cast, with candidates drawn from party lists. In electoral systems with PR, it should also be noted that voter turn-out is generally higher than in those which have SMPS. In the British SMPS, the fact that only 35 MPs (all Labour Party) were elected by over 50 per cent of the voters in their constituencies raises the question of whether many votes are wasted, with the result that many electors might feel disenfranchised. This appears to be a factor in why many citizens are more active in informal and unorthodox forms of participation.

Germany adopts the additional member system or AMS (see also **Qvortrup, 2005**), which is a hybrid of SMPS and one form of PR. In Germany we can see how the balance of power between left and right changes infrequently. In this electoral system, voters vote twice: once for their party and once for their local representative. Half of the seats in the Bundestag are elected in the same way as in the UK, that is, by citizens voting for the candidates to represent the constituency. The other half of the seats are allocated according to the proportion of votes received by each party in each region (less the number of representatives that have already been elected as constituency representatives). This allows smaller evenly spread parties such as the Greens or the Free Democrats to have representatives drawn from a party list even if they are not successful in any individual constituency. The result is a situation in which no single party predominates and both the Christian Democrats on the right and the Social Democrats on the left need the support of minor parties to form a stable government. In Germany, because of the sensitivity to neo-Nazi fringe parties, there is a threshold of support (5 per cent) which prevents some minor parties from securing seats, and hence the result is not strictly proportional.

Prior to reunification, in West Germany a 'two and a half party system' emerged whereby a combination of Christian Democrats and the small centrist Free Democrats governed from 1949 through to 1969, followed by collaboration between Social Democrats and Free Democrats until 1982 (when there was another switch of the pivotal Free Democrats to form Kohl's Christian Democrat government). There was some concern that the reunification of East and West Germany in 1990 (following the collapse of Soviet dominance in Eastern Europe) would destabilize a finely balanced system which had worked admirably since the 1950s. In particular, the relationship between parties and the electorate could be transformed by the inclusion of former East German citizens and their unpredictable political affiliations. The Free Democrats, Social Democrats and Christian Democrats all merged with their East German counterparts (though the mergers were weighted in favour of the Western German political parties), followed later by the former Communist Party in East Germany (rebranded as the PDS) taking over the smaller group of West German communists. The Greens were the only major political party not to seek a merger.

Both the electoral and party systems operated in such a way as to stabilize the new political system and foster the emerging civil society in the former East Germany, though not without a few teething problems. The Federal Constitutional Court decided that the East and West should be separate voting areas for this one election, to ensure that parties located mainly in East Germany did not have to achieve the minimum threshold necessary to achieve representation in the Bundestag (that is, just for this election the threshold would be 5 per cent of *either* the former West or East German voters according to where the parties were located, and not 5 per cent of all German voters). Otherwise, without support in West Germany the parties in East Germany would need votes from more than 23 per cent of the electorate in East Germany in order to reach the 5 per cent threshold.

In effect, this worked against the Greens. The Greens of the former East Germany managed to secure two representatives in the East (as allies of citizen initiatives, the 'Alliance '90/Greens', who received eight seats in all). But the Greens competing in the constituencies of the former West Germany achieved no seats. (See Table 3.2.) Had the West Greens allied themselves with their East German counterparts, they would have achieved 5.1 per cent of the votes cast: the Greens 3.9 per cent plus the Alliance '90/Greens 1.2 per cent. They would thus have been over the 5 per cent threshold for the whole of Germany and entitled to 33 representatives (i.e. 5.1 per cent of the 662 total seats, shown in Table 3.2). While the 5 per cent barrier distorts the results in proportional terms – there were still 8.1 per cent of the votes overall which did not result in a preferred candidate being elected – this is a considerably smaller share of 'wasted' votes than in SMPS, where most constituencies elect a representative on less than 50 per cent of the votes cast. In addition, these 8.1 per cent of the seats are redistributed to the other parties who are over the 5 per cent threshold.

TABLE 3.2   Share of the votes in the reunification election for the Bundestag, 1990

Party	All Germany (%)	West Germany (%)	East Germany (%)	Total seats
*(CDU/CSU/FDP, the governing coalition)	(54.8)	(54.9)	(54.7)	(398)
*CDU (Christian Democratic Union)	36.7	35.5	41.8	268
*CSU (Christian Social Union)	7.1	8.8	–	51
*FDP (Free Democratic Party)	11.0	10.6	12.9	79
SPD (Social Democratic Party)	33.5	35.7	24.3	239
Greens	3.9	4.8	0.1	0
Alliance '90/Greens	1.2	–	6.0	8
PDS (Party of Democratic Socialism)	2.4	0.3	11.1	17
Republicans	2.1	2.3	1.3	0
Greys	0.8	0.8	0.8	0
Others	1.3	1.2	1.7	0
			Total seats:	662

Source: Federal Returning Officer, 2004

Elsewhere in Western European societies, strong identification with one of numerous political parties has been combined with the operation of electoral systems based on proportional representation. This ensured that many European societies witnessed long periods of electoral stability but with a range of political parties, none of whom could command a majority on their own. In many cases, this led parties to build alliances and form coalition governments. Even though many countries have experienced frequent elections, this does not necessarily lead to instability. In Italy, having elections every one or two years created a mechanism for the partners in a coalition to establish their level of popular support and adjust the allocation of ministerial positions to each party. The biggest danger was that of *immobilism*: whenever a majority was constructed no one could agree on policy, and whenever a policy was agreed a majority did not exist – a recipe for political crisis. Another drawback is that coalitions are constructed through backroom deals and horse-trading between different parties, so no electors get what they really want. In the UK, then, at least some groups of electors have a government which can claim to represent their views and values. Table 3.3 provides an overview of the various types of electoral systems.

TABLE 3.3 Variety of electoral systems

	Single member plurality system (SMPS)	Additional member system (AMS)	Party list	Single transferable vote (STV)	Alternative vote (AV)
Method for selecting representatives	The candidate with the most votes wins the seat (single member constituencies).	Some seats are allocated to candidates with the most votes for constituency representation using SMPS, while the remainder of seats are drawn from party lists in each region to ensure that the final distribution of seats corresponds to parties' share of the overall vote.	Political parties are allocated seats in direct proportion to the number of votes they receive (subject to the elimination of smaller parties which do not reach a specific threshold).	Candidates who achieve a specific quota of the vote are elected and their surplus votes redistributed to second preferences; if any seats remain unfilled, the second or even third preferences of the candidate with the lowest votes are distributed until all the seats are filled.	If a candidate does not receive more than half of the first preferences of voters, the candidate with the least votes is eliminated and voters' second preferences are redistributed until one candidate has over half the votes.
Minimum votes needed for each seat	One more vote than the nearest rival candidate (hence it is often known as 'first past the post').	One more vote than the nearest rival candidate for constituency representatives; quota from party list for the remainder.	Quota formula depending on the number of seats in the representative chamber.	Quota formula depending on the number of seats in the multi-seat constituency (usually combining the constituencies in one region).	50 per cent plus one vote.
Selecting representatives between elections	By-election.	Next candidate of the same party on that party's list.	Next candidate of the same party on that party's list.	By-election.	By-election.
Examples	the UK House of Commons, Canada	Germany, Scottish Parliament	Norway, Italy, Finland, Sweden, Israel	Republic of Ireland, Malta, Australian Senate	Australian House of Representatives

In some systems of proportional representation (see STV and AV in Table 3.3) some representatives are elected with a combination of first, second or even third preferences. It is arguable that having representatives who are most people's second or worse choice reduces the legitimacy of the process.

Another variant, the second ballot system, is different from alternative vote systems (where the second, third and so on preferences are allocated when a voter's preferred candidates are knocked out). The electoral process takes place in two discrete stages. If no candidate wins over 50 per cent of the first stage of voting, then the two candidates with the most votes go forward to the second ballot (as in the elections for the French President) or in legislative elections the candidates who secure above a specific percentage of votes (for the French legislature the minimum necessary is 12.5 per cent in an electoral district). In France, which uses SMPS with a second ballot, political parties that have widely distributed rather than concentrated support tend to do badly. Defenders of second ballot variants argue that democratic legitimacy is increased by having successful candidates who have attracted the support of over half the electorate. According to this view, democratic legitimacy would be absent if the winning candidate had significantly less than 50 per cent of the vote and just a handful more votes than defeated candidates.

The argument in favour of SMPS is that political parties can, on the whole, provide robust leadership and a clear sense of direction as they don't have to consult widely (in the way that coalition governments have to do). The key argument against SMPS is that the national assembly or parliament does not provide a fair reflection of the views of the electorate, both as individuals and as different sectors of societies.

Whether we would prefer effectiveness or fairness, no electoral system is perfect and each has its own peculiar effects in translating mass voting into political representation. For example, many countries with proportional representation have a threshold (in Germany this is 5 per cent), which prevents smaller parties from achieving representation. But this can impact upon all smaller parties – as in the case of the Greens in some recent elections in Germany.

The problem in defining participation is really a matter of the variety of ways in which individuals and groups can make their demands and needs felt within political institutions and processes. In the *societal* sense, political parties are electoral coalitions which, if successful, play a role in forging broad agreement across distinctive sections of society by attracting people towards a common policy platform and thus mobilize resources for political projects. Generally, these are not static but fluid coalitions which adapt to changing circumstances. This is a response to the combined peculiarities of:

- the political and ideological values at work in the cultural context

- the distinctive political parties in existence

- the electoral system in place.

We have acknowledged that there is no such thing as a perfect electoral system or party system, just those which are more or less well suited to the society in question. In the next section, we will investigate one case (Zimbabwe) of how, in very complex circumstances, an electoral system did not contribute to the development of stable or inclusive democratic rule.

SUMMARY

- The bases of political participation have changed as new group identities emerged in the course of social change.

- When comparing participation in different countries (such as the UK and Germany) with party systems based on similar ideological and policy conflicts, the precise form of electoral system can produce very different kinds of outcomes.

- Some electoral systems generate victories for minority political parties in order to enable decisive leadership; others are more inclusive of the range of interests and demands of different social groups.

6 PROBLEMS OF ELECTORAL PARTICIPATION: THE ZIMBABWEAN CASE

This case study has been included to highlight the importance of thinking about the relationship between electoral system participation, party politics and political culture, as well as considering the formal mechanism for translating voting support into representatives in the national assembly. Electoral systems operate in specific contexts, and a system which fosters inclusiveness and social peace in one country may provoke disaffection and turmoil in another. Of course, neither a legitimate, accepted electoral system nor one which divides a people can, on its own, be blamed for social and political instability. It will always be one factor among many others. Nevertheless, we can point to examples where an electoral system which has had positive effects in one place has had quite the opposite in another.

Consider in this context the case of Zimbabwe. In recent years, democracy has seen considerable advance in Africa, not least in South Africa with the end of the apartheid regime. But it is certainly true that many African societies have suffered unstable and authoritarian governments in the last 40 years and, while the causes are complex, there is evidence that the systems of political representation established as part of the end of imperial control have contributed to this unhappy history.

With regard to Zimbabwe, the 1979 Lancaster House Agreement, following the peace agreement between the white Rhodesian rulers and the black resistance movements, meant that a British-style parliamentary system was implemented in 1980. There were two very important institutional differences, however. First, to safeguard the interests of the white minority – who had formerly been the only individuals granted political rights – the existing rights to land ownership were guaranteed by the principle that land could only change hands when there was a willing buyer and willing seller. Second, a mechanism of disproportionate representation was introduced, whereby 20 per cent of the parliamentary seats were allocated to parties competing for the white vote for the first term of parliament, with a fully fledged SMPS from 1985.

The land reform issue, a long standing grievance for many Zimbabwean citizens, was off the agenda; 99.4 per cent of the population (the black majority) had access to 30 per cent of the land while 0.6 per cent of the population owned 70 per cent of the land (including most known mineral deposits). This inequality was reinforced by the poor agricultural quality of land for the majority. In this way, an undercurrent of disaffection over the land issue among the majority presented huge challenges for an electoral mechanism to cope with.

Like many decolonized societies, Zimbabwe is a plural society with significant cultural divisions, in this case between the minority Nbelele and the majority Shona ethnic groups. These divisions became manifest in the national liberation movement in the 1970s and surfaced in the formation of political parties – ZANU-PF (Robert Mugabe's political base in Shona regions) and ZAPU (Joshua Nkomo's base in Ndebele regions, largely in Matabeleland). From 1980 and as a result of SMPS, ZANU secured a majority of seats in elections and, in a bid to prevent violent regional and tribal strife between the supporters of the two parties, the leaders unified the two parties in 1988. In this situation, multi-party democracy was sacrificed to quell unrest. SMPS reinforced the overwhelming parliamentary majority of ZANU. Further, the simmering land issue began to undermine the broader democratic system. The failure to successfully address the land issue meant that the increasingly authoritarian Mugabe government has used compulsory land seizures and the promise of future land reform to mobilize sufficient popular support despite violations of human rights, a compromised judiciary and severe economic depression.

The complicated history of Zimbabwe cannot be fully covered here, though we will return to the implications of dissent in this context later in the chapter. Nevertheless, this brief overview provides insights into some of the difficulties that emerge when a system of political representation operates on an economic, political and cultural situation as part of an international agreement but one with limited domestic support. Normally a mechanism designed to generate political stability and legitimacy, reconciling the diverse interests of citizens in a society, the electoral system in Zimbabwe has failed to achieve these objectives. Electoral systems have to be designed in a way that provides ample opportunities for participation, so that citizens feel that their grievances and concerns are understood and acted upon. Comparative analysis also has to take due account of the different contexts of political systems.

The next section considers the variety of ways in which social movements and pressure groups operate as mediating mechanisms for political participation. Here we will also examine how parties have been challenged by group politics.

- Electoral systems can lead to different consequences depending on the political and cultural context.
- Some institutional mechanisms for participation can generate crisis and instability.

7 IN AND AGAINST THE GROOVE: PARTICIPATION AND DISSENT

At this point we return to the relation between participation and dissent. Earlier we highlighted how participation involves a combination of assent and dissent, and that both activities can be beneficial for democratic governance. Here we focus more explicitly on those who challenge the way politics is conducted and the policies and decisions that arise from the deliberations of political institutions. Sometimes this can involve critical interventions within the usual political channels, but dissent can go much further than this to undermine the 'normal' social and political values that sustain them.

Dissenters often propose very different *ends* or objectives for society which challenge what passes for political common sense and its taken-for-granted assumptions. These objectives can sometimes be pursued by living a different kind of life based on alternative values (such as those of the commune movement), but they can also manifest themselves by challenging the normal political *means* (such as the usual mechanisms for participation already outlined). Dissenters can mobilize around alternative political means ranging from orderly protests and demonstrations to armed struggle and terrorism.

7.1   Group variations

We will start by focusing on groups which attempt to work within the political system and the role they play in making the political system work. To this end we shall explore the difference between interest groups and promotional groups, before considering whether they become incorporated into or are marginalized within the system (in other words, becoming 'insiders' or 'outsiders').

Group politics comes in many forms and, as a start, it is useful to classify their activities. If we consider their relationship to the society they inhabit, some groups seek to conserve the status quo (confirmatory participation) while others seek to change existing social and political structures; whether we should describe this as reformist participation or transformist participation depends on the extent and kind of change involved.

Reformist groups work within the existing rules of the political system to change the minds of electors, press for amendments in legislation and affect the implementation of policies. Transformist groups are more suspicious of the institutions through which offending policies are produced (as well as the motives of the politicians and civil servants who produce them). Not only do they want to change attitudes and specific policies, they seek to challenge the operation of the political system itself and often redefine what is considered to be a political issue. For example, feminist movements treat domestic violence as a political issue rather than a private matter or personal issue.

Since groups are politically purposive, we can begin by contrasting the following two types of pressure groups.

- *Interest groups*
  These groups defend the sectional interests of their members, acting as the voice for specific aggregates of individuals with, for example, a common occupational and/or financial position, as is the case for *Italia Nostra* (heritage organization, Italy), the British Medical Association (professional association, the UK), and the Confederation of Entrepreneurial Organizations (business association, Spain). Interest groups often provide a range of functions for their members which are not directly related to influencing politics.

- *Promotional groups*
  These groups promote a particular cause, a purpose which does not usually correspond to the social position of the members, for example GeneEthics (against GMOs, Australia), National Right to Life Committee (the USA), Shelter (supporting the homeless, the UK), Greenpeace, and the Danish Demining Group. These groups can also include campaigning charitable groups, such as Live Aid and Sport Relief.

No classifications of groups in politics are straightforward. It is worth making some further distinctions. First, we can distinguish between groups whose participation is 'confirmatory' (broadly aimed at retaining the status quo), and those whose participation is intended to be 'reformist' (challenging the status quo). In truth, many groups participate in political systems in both of these ways though, for example, a group such as Greenpeace is largely reformist and one such as the British Medical Association largely confirmatory.

Second, groups can adopt different strategies. They might, for example, focus their efforts and resources on convincing the government or MPs or local councillors – officials in the 'system'. On the other hand, they might concentrate their efforts on changing attitudes and sometimes lifestyles of people in general.

Third, and very importantly, some groups become insiders and others outsiders, or they are treated as such by governments. There are certain benefits to being insiders in the political process at an early stage, benefits that come from helping to define the ways in which political issues arise and how they are implemented. Indeed, they may actually be the main agency through which policies are put into action while other groups are excluded from such partnership arrangements. Outsider groups often benefit from having the virtuous standpoint of not having to share the responsibility for the consequences of such policies (leading to the accusation that they are professional dissenters). Some groups can choose to be insiders or outsiders; others have these roles thrust upon them, so to speak.

7.2 Power: inclusion and exclusion

The most powerful groups are insiders and these are usually the least heard about publicly. In some cases, where governments already endorse the interests of specific groups (such as the biotechnology industry or the financial sector), the groups don't even have to engage in political action. Evidence of this symbiosis of interest can be seen in the appointment of former ministers and higher civil servants to consultancy posts or to part-time executive positions in specific companies and in the inclusion of specific groups in the formation and implementation of policy. In these situations, policy makers need the information such groups provide in order to devise effective policy frameworks that can be implemented in a way which would achieve the desired outcomes. Most of these privileged groups also employ lobbying consultants to enhance their capacity to have an impact on the successive drafts of legislation, in order to create a regulative context that is broadly supportive of the interests involved. It is not always the case that groups that have been included in the past continue to be included in the future. Rural interests now feel excluded from policy making (as Figure 3.3 illustrates).

FIGURE 3.3   The return of the mass demonstration. *Left:* in September 2002, 400,000 people supported the Countryside Alliance demonstration for 'liberty and livelihood' (against proposed anti-hunting legislation and in defence of rural interests); *right:* in February 2003, one million marched against military intervention in Iraq in London

Groups can therefore contribute to the quality of democracy by providing specialized and contextual knowledge on the issues at hand, representing the marginalized and powerless whose views would not otherwise be heard, throwing a spotlight on the real effects of policies, opening up discussion on difficult topics and generally improving the quality of political deliberation. Of course, questions can be asked about the motives of unaccountable political campaigners and whether some groups exert an unfair influence, such as the insider groups referred to earlier. Table 3.5 summarizes the implications of the activities of these different groupings – hindering or helping – in the democratic process.

TABLE 3.5 Do groups hinder or help democracy?

Pressure groups hinder democracy!	Pressure groups help democracy!
Pressure groups have a varying amount of influence and some sections of society are more adequately represented than others. Some groups representing business and professional interests are strong, while those representing consumers, the elderly, the unemployed and migrants are usually less influential (as a result of organizational factors it is easier to coordinate manufacturing organizations than consumers).	Pressure groups facilitate political participation for all citizens but in particular for the vast majority of citizens who are not members of political parties (with participation taking active forms or more passive forms such as cheque book participation). Since parties no longer effectively integrate citizens into the political system, groups and movements are now vitally important.
Some groups are affiliated closely with specific political parties so there is a danger that they receive preferential treatment when that political party is in power while other groups lose out. There is also the danger that groups are so closely integrated that they become a means of achieving government policy against the interests of their members (such as unions imposing pay restraint on their members).	Pressure groups often have access to the detailed information that is crucial to policy makers devising policies and initiatives that will achieve desired objectives. These groups are consulted, for they provide useful channels of communication for governments. Such pressure groups specialize in particular policy areas, acquiring a substantial level of expertise which can improve policy proposals and propose alternatives.
The leaders of pressure groups are usually appointed rather than elected. In addition, the decision making of pressure groups often lacks transparency and the leaders rarely have to justify their actions to their members or the wider public.	Pressure groups keep a close check on the activities of governments in areas of policy and administration that affect their members or are relevant to the cause they promote. They can act as whistle-blowers and draw attention to the unintended consequences of specific policy proposals.

The question of the relative power of competing groups in influencing governments is a difficult one. The success of group activity is not easy to measure. We can identify the development of legislation and policy initiatives that serve the interests of specific groups (for instance, business associations), but this is the exception rather than the rule. Many groups with diffuse membership, such as those representing consumers, find it hard to counter the effectiveness of the relatively small number of producers. The numerical difference between consumers and productive organizations presents distinctive logistical difficulties for representing the interests of consumers, but situations can emerge (such as a health crisis or pollution event) where public opinion will ensure that consumer interests achieve a higher degree of prominence. What we can conclude is that power and influence are related both to access to policy-making communities and to the capacity of a group to mobilize resources for exerting an influence.

The methods used to exert pressure and influence are various and usually used in combination, but the precise mix of methods generally relates closely to their insider/outsider status. Leaflet and poster dissemination in order to publicize interests or a cause often works best with local campaigns, though it usually features as part of the mix of methods in broader group activities. Demonstrations, especially if large, can act as a 'wake-up-call' to policy communities, signalling that a group has been ignored but, on the whole, such events are a symptom of a lack of influence and the primary function is the boost to the morale of group members.

Careful use of the media is often seen as the blood supply for groups in attempts to influence public opinion but also to raise the profile of a particular group in the eyes of legislators and government ministers. These methods are the primary ones for outsider groups, although they may be combined with direct action tactics (to which we shall return below when focusing on dissenting groups). Most effective (associated with insider groups) is direct involvement in political parties, lobbying parliament and acquiring access to senior civil servants and ministers (with the latter as the Holy Grail as a result of the shift of power from the legislative to the executive branches of government).

Given the increased participation in group activities and the corresponding decline in membership of political parties, there is some concern that groups are not always organized democratically. This has concerned heritage associations which have traditionally been concerned with environmental conservation, such as the German Federation for Environment and Nature Protection (BUND) or the National Trust in the UK, as well as animal welfare groups, such as the RSPCA. Since the 1990s, members of anti-hunt and anti-vivisection groups have joined these organizations and attempted to change their stance regarding the treatment of animals. Such 'group wars' are evident in an internal power struggle, in this case, over whether hunting with dogs should be allowed on the land owned by these organizations.

7.3 Disobedience strategies

So far we have focused on classifying group activities and considering how their political strategies can be seen as a response to whether they are included in or excluded from the usual mechanisms of political participation. Later, we shall focus on those groups that challenge the *ends* and/or the *means* of the political system in more radical ways. Some groups are willing to engage in a wider range of activities which involve civil disobedience. As should be becoming clear, dissent is more than just one kind of participation (Figure 3.4).

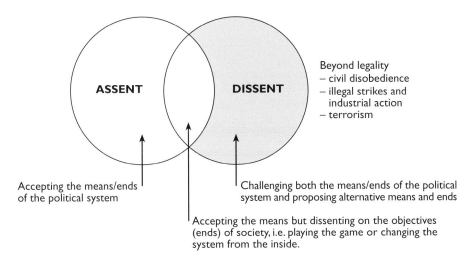

FIGURE 3.4   Participation: the combination of both assent and dissent, but not all dissent is participation

Protest groups engage in strategies of dissent which differ in quite fundamental ways from the examples highlighted so far. Of course, many groups are capable of the kinds of dissent that involve breaking laws. The physical obstruction of public spaces or chaining oneself to the railings outside public buildings has been a feature of protest from the time of the women's suffrage movement in the early twentieth century, through to the peace movement of the 1950s to the 1980s, and the protests by disability activists in the 1990s. These groups are likely to be less organizationally coherent and often involve a collection of groups affiliated together as a social movement. Whereas most pressure groups tend to accept the formal rules of political participation and seek to change policies and laws by parliamentary means, new social movements are often willing to engage in extra-parliamentary action and civil disobedience. This is usually justified by reference to what they consider to be higher principles of human rights. In effect, it means that the political institutions of a specific society lack legitimacy.

The point of such movements is not only to stop, for example, the deployment of particular weapons or introduce anti-discrimination laws, but also to alter the taken-for-granted common sense that underpins the political system in which they live. They seek to change the attitudes and values of the public and, where their activities are suppressed by the police (occasionally with the help of the armed forces), are more willing to challenge the existing institutional arrangements of the political system. For example, anarchist groups view the democratic institutions of liberal societies as an expression of a fundamental misunderstanding of the idea of freedom. Rather than viewing representative democracy as a sensible mechanism for aggregating the diverse views and interests of mass societies, for anarchists the idea that citizens elect people to make decisions for them is an abdication of responsibility for governing one's own affairs. Instead, they propose that political organizations should involve direct democracy (which implies smaller scale political institutions) and the principle that all officials (including judges and civil servants) should be revocable at any time.

Some movements such as feminist and environmental movements have attempted to develop less elitist forms of political organization, based on rotating leaderships, delegations and 'group consciousness-raising'. The latter, developed in the feminist movement of the 1960s and 1970s, involves sharing personal experiences so that one's personal experiences of oppression can be recognized as part of a system of oppression. In this sense, the personal becomes political (assuming that power relations operate in private life and in the attitudes and values that underpin our actions as well as in the context of public politics of the national assembly and government).

In one interesting experiment, Green parties adopted such non-elitist forms of political organization. Rather than the party conference being geared to set-piece speeches and adulation of the leadership, the party conferences were more informal events structured around small group discussions, nicknamed 'table talk'. After initial electoral success, the Green parties went through a series of internal debates on whether to stick to these fundamental principles (but ones which made it difficult to respond to fast-moving politics) or adopt a more conventional party structure and leadership arrangement. In the end, they opted for a realistic party structure though, in the process, they lost members who had joined the Greens to change the way politics was conducted.

On practical strategies for change, the focus of such movements is much more on local and single issues. The feminist movement can claim some success in changing attitudes to domestic violence and sexual assaults though the necessary institutional changes to judicial and policing practices and the operation of social services have taken decades. It is often remarked that changing political attitudes and values is a multi-generational strategy rather than something that can be fixed by legislation or a short-term government initiative.

7.4 Violent and non-violent acts

Most forms of civil disobedience are non-violent and this is explicitly justified by either acknowledging that the coercive arm of the state is much too strong to make violence realistic or, more positively, by drawing on the tradition of passive resistance developed by Tolstoy, Gandhi, Martin Luther King and Jesse Jackson. This assertion of non-violence as a moral principle in politics (often tied to religious values) places an emphasis on mutual love and respect (note the recent incarnations of this kind of movement, the fluffies, in Figure 3.5). The tradition was still evident in the rhetoric of the peaceful mass demonstration against the Iraq War in London in 2003 where the members of the demonstration were invoked by Jesse Jackson to 'give peace a chance, give hope a chance'. Civil disobedience involves a defiant action that deliberately breaks the law and an acceptance that such actions will invoke a punishment: protesters should conduct themselves with dignity, quietly accepting the actions of the police or military. The objective is to highlight the coercive operation of the state in defending an unjust law as well as to generate media coverage of the issue. Once imprisoned for public disorder offences, some protesters have gone on to engage in hunger strikes.

Groups like these have also engaged in direct action tactics (in the example of The Land is Ours campaign, the occupation of brown-field sites often involves committing an illegal trespass). Direct action tactics can involve nuisance protests, such as Greenpeace dumping a large amount of soil outside a government office (with an erroneous claim that it contained anthrax, to prompt a terrorist alert) or attempting to block the pipelines emitting industrial effluent from a chemical factory in Workington or the removal of nuclear waste from Sellafield nuclear power station.

However, we should be careful not to assume that these forms of political protest are always associated with leftist groups. Neo-Nazi political parties and looser groupings of fascists continue to engage in low-level political violence. French farmers have engaged in public protests to prevent changes in agricultural policy. Similarly in the UK, farmers and haulage operators have blockaded highways, oil-refineries and petrol stations. More recently, the Countryside Alliance has brought together a wide rural lobby on farming subsidies, hunting and deteriorating local services, to organize national demonstrations and more localized acts of protest including blocking highways. These are usually to prevent change rather than promote it, but are often a symptom that a particular community has felt threatened by a variety of changes over a considerable length of time and is anxious to air its concerns.

In some cases, when citizens break the law for political ends, violence and even terror can be manifested (note the spikies in Figure 3.5 and their contrast with the fluffies). This may take the form of destruction of property (the Anti-Poll Tax Rally, Trafalgar Square, London, 1990), though in news coverage the actions of opportunist criminals are often confused with the protest. Some groups have become so frustrated with the more conventional forms of political participation, they have used violence to intimidate individuals and prevent organizations from engaging in certain activities, such as the retailing of animal furs or experimentation on animals (which can only continue under conditions of high security). The Animal Liberation Front has engaged in illegal entry into laboratory facilities, the 'liberation' of animals from farms (such as mink farms) and occasionally the car bombing of laboratory scientists. These kinds of strategies for political action have been borrowed from groups such as the Red Army Faction, Action Direct and the IRA, though they have not deployed a wide range of bomb devices, home-made mortar attacks, assassinations and short-range missiles.

Political organizations involved in the use of violence can also deploy non-violent forms of protest, as illustrated in the use of 'dirty protests' (smearing excrement and urine) and hunger strikes in an attempt to obtain 'prisoner of

The spikies

Manifesto

Capitalism perpetrates violence, so violence against property and persons is perfectly justifiable in the cause of anti-capitalism. A few more festivals of broken glass in central London and the entire capitalist machine will grind swiftly to a halt, to be replaced with, um, can we get back to you on that one?

How to spot them

Balaclavas to prevent identification by the police – a cunning distraction, say the fluffies, many of whom reckon they are state-planted *agents provocateur* in any case.

Favoured tactics

Gutting the Gap, smashing Starbucks, mangling McDonald's. "Their aim is violence against police officers," said one police officer; nevertheless, they are arguably less confusing to the police since they presumably have some ringleaders (Osama bin Laden? Phil Mitchell?) – unlike the fluffies.

Classic campaign

The Battle of Seattle, when a mob of violent protesters looted shops and clashed with riot police.

Key accessory

The brick.

Historical antecedents

Violent ideologues from crusaders to Eta.

Names they go by

Anarchist Federation, Urban Alliance.

Spikies on fluffies

"Sad to see the idiots . . . standing in front of the lines of tooled-up riot cops shouting 'No, no, don't throw things, we're here to party' – a 1997 leaflet released by the spiky-led "Hungry Brigade".

Embarrassing media figurehead

Matthew MacDonald, an Eton schoolboy whose efforts to bring down the Establishment from the inside were cut swiftly short when he was arrested for hurling a chair through the window of a central London branch of the multinational McDonald's.

Cunning disguise . . . spiky uniform

The fluffies

Manifesto

You can't fight violence with violence: non-violent direct action is the only way to confront an inherently violent economic system.

How to spot them

Unmasked faces, whistles on ribbons, bright costumes, distressing facial hair.

Favoured tactics

Guerrilla gardening, street parties; fire-breathing, marching into police lines with battering rams made of foam – a particular favourite of the White Overall Movement Building Liberation Through Effective Struggle, or Wombles. Also: spending too much valuable anti-capitalist campaigning time coming up with comedy acronyms.

Classic campaign

Operation Dessert Storm, deploying custard pies in the service of anarchy. "What better way to draw attention to the often faceless leaders of the corporate world, shameful 'journalists', dodgy politicians and anyone who deserves a full face of dissent? The 'global movement' is often misrepresented in the mainstream media. You can't misrepresent a face full of cream."

Key accessory

Penny whistle.

Historical antecedents

Non-violent direct action from Mahatma Gandhi to the hippies to Ya Basta!, the Italian non-violent support group for the Zapatistas who pioneered the dastardly "foam battering ram" method.

Names they go by

Reclaim the Streets, Mayday Collective.

Spikies on fluffies

"The fluffy-spiky debate has become a cliche, and is filed under The Great Unmentionables, along with Swampy – [but] if we use violence, we give the vested interests something more interesting to talk about. They get away with carrying on, and usually with a lot more support" – fluffy campaigner.

Embarrassing media figurehead

Swampy, the tree-dwelling hero of Newbury bypass action.

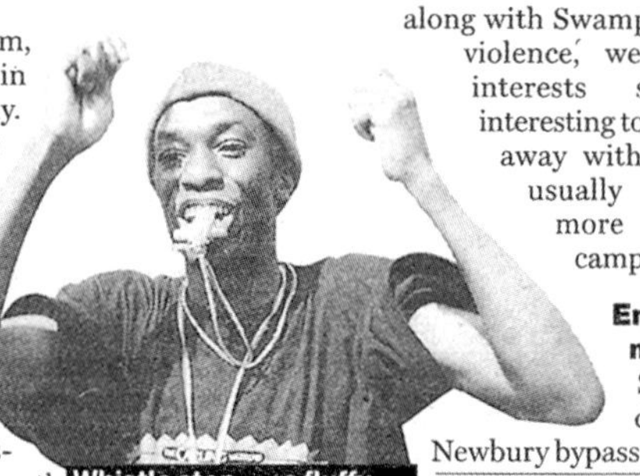

Whistle stop . . . a fluffy

FIGURE 3.5

Resistance variations: anti-party types

war' status within the Maze high security prison in Northern Ireland. Indeed, the Irish republican prisoners involved achieved considerable publicity and international sympathy from these actions despite the deaths that resulted (cases include that of Bobby Sands who was elected as an MP shortly before his death). The return to a relative peace in Northern Ireland also indicates that violence is not necessarily automatically associated with certain forms of politics. Examples of former 'terrorists' becoming national political leaders (Mandela in South Africa is one) does raise difficult questions for advocates of peaceful participation.

In Europe and North America, where traditions of dissent have been long established, protest and civil disobedience is met on the whole with considerable restraint by the coercive arm of the state (the police, army and judiciary). In other societies, dissent can place in danger the life of an active citizen (and that of their friends and family). Earlier, we considered the undermining of multi-party democracy in Zimbabwe. As a result of the economic and political crises in Zimbabwe, for example, a political movement has emerged which seeks to challenge the dominance of the Mugabe government. The Movement for Democratic Reform (established in 2000) has sought to challenge the ZANU's candidates at elections in the face of intimidation and violence directed at the key members of the movement as well as through national general strikes and mass protests. In response, the regime has mobilized the National Liberation War Veterans Association (with promises of land acquisition) to control the emergent democratic movement through political violence, resulting in the deaths of key MDR activists and their sympathizers in the trade unions and student organizations. Given that many countries are intolerant of dissent, civil disobedience can involve a considerable sacrifice in authoritarian contexts (Figure 3.6). We can see, then, that while comparisons can be useful, we also have to be careful to consider protest movements in the very different contexts in which they take place.

7.5 Experimental politics

Aside from these examples, the forms of political activity that involve protest usually attempt to challenge the organization of politics and society in fundamental ways but do so largely peacefully. They often operate at the sub-political level rather than focusing on established political institutions. The Land is Ours campaign (which you met earlier in the chapter) is a useful illustration of this. The campaign involves taking over brown-field sites in cities and setting up prototype villages that demonstrate an alternative lifestyle based on ecological principles ('politics by example'), but also makes the substantive point that brown-field sites are being neglected in favour of building homes, supermarkets and industrial estates in green locations.

Social movements are thus cultural laboratories for new lifestyles and values, often existing as latent currents in cultural relations and only manifest in visible outbursts at certain times. Since the 1960s various social movements have

FIGURE 3.6   The ultimate political sacrifice: a Buddhist monk protests against government persecution of Buddhists, Saigon, 1963

emerged which are not rooted in social class. These have focused on the discrimination and inequalities that emerge from sexual preference, gender and ethnic identity. While such movements have deployed conventional methods for exerting influence, they can also be understood as 'submerged networks'. Such social movements have been described as *pre-political* because they derive sustenance from everyday life, as well as *meta-political* because while their interests can be represented they can never be fully captured by political parties or conventional interest and promotional groups (Melucci, 1989). New patterns of dissent pose a challenge to the way we think about what constitutes a legitimate form of political participation in modern democracies.

SUMMARY

- The power and influence of groups can be used to keep political institutions in touch with the concerns of citizens between elections, but not when certain groups are able to capture specific areas of policy.

- The political strategies of groups and social movements raise single issues more effectively than political parties do, and develop novel solutions to political and social problems.

- If politics involves power relations then a focus on established political institutions is not sufficient for understanding political participation in new social movements.

- We need to focus our attention much more on the *politics of the personal* if we are to grasp the complex mixtures of participation and dissent in liberal democracies.

8 CONCLUSION: RETHINKING PARTICIPATION AND DISSENT

In contemporary liberal democracies, it is clear that citizens feel more disengaged from core political processes and alienated from the centres of political power. Instead of indicating an end to politics, it may be that this heralds a widening and diversification of the politics of participation, that public politics is being replaced by the politics of the personal? While there is some evidence that many groups are more willing to engage in single issue politics and forms of protest, this appears to indicate that there are more opportunities for political participation, rather than any widespread apathy or forms of political actions that oppose liberal democracy itself. Few studies of informal and unorthodox forms of participation have been conducted in the past and the Citizen Audit is part of a refocusing of research in this area of political studies. As we saw earlier, the audit reveals forms of low-level political activism which may have existed for a long time and have simply gone unnoticed.

What can we conclude about political participation? First, focusing on formal and orthodox forms of political participation, such as voting in elections and membership of political parties, misses many other kinds of participation. Unorthodox participation based on informal local and voluntary networks that support specific groups of people or redress grievances on issues such as educational and health services are just as important.

Second, political participation is culturally and historically specific. Attention should be devoted to the ways in which parties and groups operate in electoral systems; these are often unique institutional arrangements in each country. While we can identify general trends, such as the prevalence of coalition governments in political systems that have some form of electoral system based on proportional representation, there is enormous variety in the effects that electoral systems can have on party politics and in ensuring that the voices of citizens can be heard.

Third, when explaining trends in political participation, the distinctions between political parties and pressure groups and between interest groups and promotional groups are analytically useful for identifying the kinds of participation that can take place. However, in practice, parties and groups work closely together and different kinds of groups often pursue a mixture of goals.

Finally, it is often assumed that effective democratic politics depends on the operation of a stable party system. Yet, recent trends toward greater participation in groups and movements in well-established liberal democracies (as well as the experience in post-communist Eastern Europe) suggest that the

FIGURE 3.7 A visible manifestation of dissent: 'The tank monument built in Prague in 1945 to mark the arrival of the Soviet army in Czechoslovakia was painted pink at the weekend and a model finger glued on top of it' (*Independent*, 30 April 1991)

maintenance of stable democracy is more to do with citizens feeling that the political system they inhabit is responsive to their concerns and is capable of managing the tensions and conflicts that can emerge in any political culture.

We have also found that many forms of dissent can be seen as a form of political participation: one may participate in order to assent or dissent. However, dissent is a kind of political activity that reflects the inability of political institutions to accommodate the competing demands of different groups. The presence of dissent, however, should not always be associated with the failure of a political system. Indeed, the visibility of dissent (as a legitimate political activity) indicates the level of tolerance of the political system in which it takes place. We should bear in mind that in some societies, dissent can be regarded as a threat to a social and political order rather than a positive contribution to a tradition of critical thinking about politics. When dissent is suppressed for long periods of time it can explode in 'provocative action' (see Figure 3.7).

What is clear is that to aid our understanding we need to look closely at the context in which the participation and dissent take place.

REFERENCES

Dahl, R.A. (1971) *Polyarchy*, New Haven, Yale University Press.

Dahl, R.A. (1989) *Democracy and its Critics*, New Haven, Yale University Press.

Federal Returning Officer (2004) *Results of the elections to the 12th German Bundestag on 2 December 1990*, Federal Statistical Office, Germany, www.bundeswahleiter.de/wahlen/ergebalt/e/t/bt-int90.htm (accessed 20 April 2004).

Franklin, M.N. (2004) *Voter Turnout and the Dynamics of Electoral Competition*, Cambridge, Cambridge University Press.

Gill, G. (2000) *The Dynamics of Democratization: Elites, Civil Society and the Transition Process*, London, Macmillan.

Lewis, P.G. (2001) 'The third wave of democracy in Eastern Europe', *Party Politics*, vol.7, no.5, pp.543–65.

Mair, P. and van Biezen, I. (2001) 'Party membership in twenty European democracies 1980–2000', *Party Politics*, vol.7, no.1, pp.5–21.

Melucci, A. (1989) *Nomads of the Present*, London, Radius.

Qvortrup, M. (2005) 'Citizens and politics: modes of participation and dissent' in Heffernan, R. and Thompson, G.F. (eds) *Politics and Power in the UK*, Edinburgh, Edinburgh University Press/The Open University.

Seyd, P., Whiteley, C. and Pattie, C. (2001) 'Citizenship in Britain: attitudes and behaviour' in Crick, B. (ed.) *Citizens: Towards a Citizenship Culture*, Oxford, Blackwell.

The Electoral Commission (2002) *Election 2001: The Official Results, The Electoral Commission*, www.electoralcommission.org.uk/elections/2001report.cfm (accessed 20 April 2004).

FURTHER READING

Dahl, R.A. (1989) *Democracy and its Critics*, New Haven, Yale University Press.

Mair, P. and van Biezen, I. (2001) 'Party membership in twenty European democracies 1980–2000', *Party Politics*, vol.7, no.1, pp.5–21.

Seyd, P., Whiteley, C. and Pattie, C. (2001) 'Citizenship in Britain: attitudes and behaviour' in Crick, B. (ed.) *Citizens: Towards a Citizenship Culture*, Oxford, Blackwell.

Common citizenship and plural identities: the politics of social difference

Judith Squires

Equality & difference

Contents

1 INTRODUCTION

The capacity to live with difference is, in my view, the coming question of the twenty-first century.

(Hall, 1993, p.361)

Citizenship has become a central political issue in recent times. This chapter focuses on citizenship in Western Europe, where controversy has centred not only on the question of who should be granted citizenship status (for example, in debates about asylum seekers and refugees), but also on what full participation in the polity as a citizen entails (for example, in debates about citizenship education in the national curriculum and the public participation of socially excluded groups). Debates about citizenship access focus largely on the appropriate role of birthplace, blood-line and marital status as criteria for claiming nationality. Debates about citizenship participation focus increasingly on the appropriate balance between the rights and responsibilities of citizens.

Until relatively recently, one of the most influential approaches to the analysis of citizenship was provided by a study of the evolution of citizenship in England by T.H. Marshall in his collection of essays, *Citizenship and Social Class* (1950). He identified three components of citizenship, which he called civil, political and social, and which he associated with the institutions of the judicial system, parliamentary democracy and the welfare state respectively. Citizenship, for Marshall (1950, pp.10–11), is a set of rights enjoyed equally by each member of the society in question (see Box 4.1). The civil component of citizenship is composed of the rights necessary for individual freedom, such as the liberty of the person, freedom of speech, thought and faith, the right to own property and the right to justice. The political component of citizenship is composed of the right to participate in the exercise of political power, and the social component is composed of a range of rights from a 'right to a modicum of economic welfare and security to the right to share to the full in the social heritage and to live the life of a civilized being according to the standards prevailing in the society' (Marshall, 1950, pp.10–11). Citizenship understood in this way has redistributive implications, as citizens are entitled to benefits (such as free health care) that they may not be able to finance without state aid.

In recent times it has been common to find cultural citizenship added to this list, which expands citizenship rights to include group rights for minority ethnic and national groups to ensure the survival of these vulnerable minority groups. The group-differentiated rights may take three forms: self-government rights, which entail some form of political autonomy to ensure the survival of cultures; polyethnic rights, which include exemptions from laws that disadvantage certain cultural groups; and special representation rights, which entail measures to overcome structural barriers to the equal representation of certain cultural groups in political bodies.

 Citizenship rights

Civil

The rights necessary for individual freedom, such as the liberty of the person, freedom of speech, thought and faith, the right to own property and the right to justice.

Political

The right to participate in the exercise of political power, either as a member or an elector of the members of a body invested with political power.

Social

The right to economic welfare and security, the right to share to the full in the social heritage, the right to live the life of a civilized being according to the standards prevailing in the society.

Cultural

The right to have one's national and ethnic differences accommodated and recognized, which may entail self-government rights, polyethnic rights or special representation rights.

Each of these elements of citizenship has become an area of central political debate. Many people have criticized the inclusion of social rights within citizenship models. Others have rejected the move to include cultural or group rights. Meanwhile 'communitarians' have influentially suggested that we need to correct the entire imbalance between rights and responsibilities, impose a moratorium on the minting of new rights, re-establish the link between rights and responsibilities and recognize that some responsibilities do not entail rights (Etzioni, 1993, p.4). Contemporary debates about citizenship therefore tend to focus on the following issues:

- *Should these rights be secured for everyone, equally?*
  Do, for example, certain cultural communities have certain group rights?

- *Who is to count as a citizen?*
  How, for example, are we to determine when asylum seekers or economic migrants should be granted citizenship?

- *Is the state responsible for citizens' social as well as civil and political rights?*
  Do citizens have a right to, for example, state-funded and state-provided health care?

- *Does the focus on rights detract attention from the fact that these rights necessarily entail correlative duties in others?*
  Does, for example, the right to be tried by a jury imply a correlative duty for one's fellow citizens to undertake jury service when called upon?

In the context of these debates about citizenship another particularly important area of contestation has emerged, focusing on the tension between demands for equality and demands that differences be recognized and affirmed. In a situation where the polity comprises very diverse groups of citizens, some of which have experienced structural and historical oppression, does a commitment to equality entail treating everyone in the same way or treating some groups differently in order to rectify previous injustices? When the polity comprises diverse communities with distinct cultural values and traditions, should the state actively ensure the survival of all these groups or should it remain passively neutral? The challenges raised by these issues are considered in Section 2.

In order to explore the ways in which states are attempting to negotiate these questions, I then go on to briefly outline and compare various contemporary European citizenship practices, in particular those of Britain, France, the Nordic countries and Belgium. The focus is on the ways in which these countries have dealt with the demands of ethnic minorities and women for greater political participation. These are taken as indicators of the citizenship practices prevalent in each of these countries, and of the recent developments within them. There are many other indicators that one could take to evaluate citizenship practices, but these are particularly helpful for comparing the different ways in which states can and do facilitate the active participation of their citizens in the polity.

Having surveyed the citizenship practices within each of these countries, as indicated by their approach to women's and ethnic minority participation, we can then assess the ways in which the countries differ from one another and evaluate their practices in the context of various theoretical models of citizenship.

2   EQUALITY AND DIVERSITY

Group representation, federalism, deliberation and e-governance are all being explored as possible strategies for redesigning democratic systems to make them more responsive to the pluralism of contemporary citizenship. The centralized, bounded and culturally homogeneous nation-state, which has for so long been assumed to be the primary political community, is widely perceived to be in need of renewal. Meanwhile, citizenship itself is gaining a new high profile, as governments attempt to respond to the increased global mobility of peoples, including economic migrants and political refugees, and the increasing diversity of their polity.

While minority groups struggle to redefine the rights of citizenship in ways that are more open to their identities, the responsibilities of citizenship are being reaffirmed by European democratic governments concerned to maintain the common political culture underpinning the nation. These governments do so against a background in which dual citizenship is becoming increasingly common, and the development of the European Union has led to the creation of legal rights from and duties to a supranational institution beyond the nation-state. Moreover, with the development of new technologies that facilitate communication and mobility, people's emotional sense of belonging is increasingly invested in non-territorial communities, which traverse the geographical boundaries of the state.

In this context, one of the central questions facing contemporary states and their citizens is how recognition of socio-cultural 'differences' can be integrated into a universal conception of citizenship that aims to secure equality for all. The idea of identity, which plays such an important role in contemporary politics, is central to what is called a 'politics of recognition'. Charles Taylor influentially defined this politics of recognition as entailing the idea that each one of us should live in a way that is true to oneself, and that this quest for authenticity should be recognized by others who have a responsibility to respect 'me' as the authentic self I think I am. What this respect entails may differ for different people. Accordingly, different people may have different rights (Taylor, 1994).

This politics of recognition issues a series of challenges to the notion of citizenship based on Marshall's vision of a socially homogeneous polity:

- Should ethnic groups, for example, give up their specific identities and assimilate into the dominant national culture, or should their distinctive cultural identity be recognized?

- Should the state establish and fund Muslim schools in order to recognize and affirm the importance of the Islamic communities within the polity, or should it insist on inclusive multifaith schools in order to ensure that all future citizens receive a common education?

- Should states actively encourage the participation of women in public life via the adoption of positive strategies to increase female candidate selection, or should it insist that all potential candidates be treated with formal equality, rendering the sex of the candidate politically non-pertinent?

States have adopted very different strategies for resolving these tensions between common citizenship and plural identities.

Equality and diversity are the twin demands made on governments by oppressed and marginalized minorities. Some want inclusion as equals within the existing legal, political and social framework; others want public recognition of their specific identities through exemptions from a legal, political and social framework they perceive to be non-neutral. Many challenge both the inequalities and injustice of contemporary societies and the exclusion and marginalization that arise from an insensitivity to difference.

The emergent preoccupation with equality and diversity raises a series of new and significant challenges to contemporary citizenship. For example, many feminists have campaigned for women's greater equality: equality of education, employment, pay and political participation. However, feminist campaigns have also been characterized by a concern to give full recognition to women's distinctive experiences and perspectives, particularly in relation to caring. Similarly, many minority ethnic groups have asserted their right to full and equal citizenship in recent years. Again, they do so both through demands for formal equality and through demands for public recognition of their cultural and religious differences.

Many people have come to argue that differences of identity, as opposed to those of interests and ideals, require an assertion of difference that poses a distinctive challenge to existing citizenship practices. This places identity and difference on the political agenda, to be negotiated alongside the commitment to equality embedded within many existing forms of citizenship. The double demand for equality and diversity appears, suggests Stuart Hall (2002, p.232), 'to outrun our existing political vocabularies'. The conundrum of how to recognize both lies at the heart of current challenges to existing citizenship practices.

SUMMARY

- Contemporary conceptions of citizenship are increasingly conditioned by the 'politics of recognition'.
- Demands for recognition of equality and diversity also offer new challenges to citizenship.

3 COMPARING WESTERN EUROPEAN CITIZENSHIP PRACTICES

There are widely opposing approaches to the study of contemporary citizenship. For example, sociologist Rogers Brubaker, in his comparative approach to citizenship and nationhood, assumes that each country has its own particular cultural idioms and national styles of thought, which structure current debates (Brubaker, 1992). According to this model, citizenship can only be understood within particular cultural idioms, and the idea of a post-national citizenship has no critical purchase. In contrast, political sociologist Yasemin Soysal suggests that all over Western Europe 'rights, participation and representation in a polity, are increasingly matters beyond the vocabulary of national citizenship' (Soysal, 1994, p.165). She points out that, since the Second World War, European states have increasingly been granting non-national residents the same social, economic and civic rights as citizens. The reason for this, she suggests, is that the state's obligations to foreigners have moved beyond the scope of the nation-state itself, and that citizenship has obtained a totally new 'post-national' character, a universal personhood (Soysal, 1994, p.142).

The limitations of the first approach lie in its tendency to foster stereotypical ideas about countries, neglecting anything that does not reinforce the assumed national culture. The limitations of the second approach lie in its lack of attention to context and the specificity of particular national histories. Moreover, both share an assumption that clear-cut patterns of thought, debate and argumentation are translated directly into policy outcomes, which is rarely the case. Given this, we need to bear in mind that these typologies and trends give only a general indication of the complexity of each state's citizenship laws and traditions. A more contextual approach allows for more nuanced insights into the complexity of contemporary citizenship.

One place to start, when comparing citizenship practices, is with nationality laws, which determine who is, and who is not, to have citizenship status. Different countries have different thresholds for citizenship, developing diverse forms of nationality laws. There are three typical bases for the granting of citizenship status: birthplace (or *jus soli*, the fact of being born in a territory), blood-line (or *jus sanguinis*, based on the nationality of parents or ancestors) and marital status (acquisition of the same citizenship as that of a spouse). Differences between nationality laws are frequently held to map on to differences among citizenship practices. States which rely on birthplace as the basis for granting citizenship status are widely held to be more inclusive and less assimilatory than states which rely on blood-line as the basis of citizenship acquisition.

It has been suggested that this produces two forms of citizenship: a political one, corresponding to territory; and a spiritual and ethnic one, based on common ancestors (Brubaker, 1992). France, for example, is frequently portrayed as an inclusive state, basing its nationality laws on birthplace; Germany is portrayed as an assimilatory state, relying on blood-line for the granting of citizenship status.

In practice, since the Second World War, nationality laws have been converging among states that perceive themselves to be democratic, stable and countries of immigration rather than emigration. First, there is a general trend towards the repeal of the right to automatic citizenship through marriage. Second, there is a convergence towards *jus soli*: in Belgium, Denmark, Finland, Italy, the Netherlands and Sweden, for example, a person born in the country to foreign parents can acquire citizenship at the age of majority after fulfilling certain residency requirements. Notably, Germany has also made a radical switch from *jus sanguinis* to *jus solis*. As of January 2000 every foreign child born in Germany whose parents either were born or have been in the country for the last eight years is automatically German at birth. This makes Germany one of the most liberal states in Europe today with regard to citizenship access. It would seem therefore that among stable, democratic countries of immigration there is a convergent guarantee of citizenship for foreign residents, linked with the idea of territorial nationality.

There may be convergence across Europe in relation to the granting of access to citizenship, but there are still significant differences among states in terms of the nature of citizenship, once acquired. This diversity can be grasped from a brief consideration of citizenship practices in Britain, France, the Nordic countries and Belgium. By adopting a comparative approach we can develop a sense of shared, transnational agendas as well as diverse national discourses, and the range of policies employed to negotiate plural identities within the polity.

One might expect a similar degree of convergence among the citizenship practices of European states: these are, after all, modern democracies, with secure borders, operating within the EU. Yet they each have quite distinctive citizenship traditions and adopt quite diverse approaches to the challenges generated by contemporary pluralism. The extent to which citizenship practices differ, even among such geographically close countries, is indicative of the broader need for careful comparative analysis.

3.1 Citizenship in Britain

Traditional British citizenship practices are perhaps best depicted by Edmund Burke in his *Reflections on the Revolution in France* (1790). Here, Burke argued that the essence of citizenship was the continuity of local groups and regional associations between the individual and the sovereign power. British practices rested on a hierarchically ordered civil society with vibrant voluntary organizations. A historical account of British citizenship practices, in contrast to the active revolutionary French citizenship, therefore reveals a polity in which rights were handed down 'from above', and where citizens were subjects with rights.

Britain was, of course, constituted by a series of conquests, invasions and settlements and its culture has long been far from unified and homogeneous. The Scottish, Welsh and Irish have always had distinctive cultures; there has been a 'black' presence in England since the sixteenth century and an Asian presence since the eighteenth century; and the distinctions between classes have been rigidly maintained through complex cultural practices. Nevertheless, modern British citizenship practices have formally (if not actually) been characterized by a determination to allow diverse cultural practices to thrive in civil society by ensuring that in the public sphere all citizens are bound by the same set of laws, a democratically elected government, and policies that regulate the economy and collective services for the common good. This public sphere exists to provide the minimum of uniformity necessary in order that individuals may conduct their private lives as they see fit.

The nature of 'Britishness', and 'Englishness', has long been on the public agenda, but especially so following Britain's turn from Empire to Europe, and the beginnings of UK devolution within the framework of the EU. The anxiety to explore the concept of Britishness has been accompanied by high-profile debates about the nature of multicultural Britain (Alibhai-Brown, 2000; Parekh, 2000). In the British context, manifestations of cultural diversity have tended to be confined to the private sphere. John Rex, for example, has argued influentially that multiculturalism is to be encouraged in the *private* sphere of personal lifestyle, marriage, family, community and religion, but is inappropriate in the *public* sphere of law, politics and the economy (Rex, 1986). This assumption is not unchallenged. One of the most important recent statements on how Britain might respond to the tensions between common citizenship and plural identities comes from The Commission on the Future of Multi-Ethnic Britain, established by the Runnymede Trust (1998–2000). The Commission analysed the current state of multi-ethnic Britain and proposed ways of ensuring that Britain could be at ease with its 'rich diversity' (Parekh, 2000, pp.vii–ix).

Significantly, members of the Commission were fundamentally committed to both equality and difference. They asserted that 'all individuals have equal worth irrespective of their colour, gender, ethnicity, religion, age or sexual orientation', which is a clear endorsement of formal equality. They also assert that 'citizens are not only individuals but also members of particular religious, ethnic, cultural and regional communities' and that Britain is a 'community of communities', which is a clear acknowledgement of the importance of difference. They attempt to square these two commitments with the suggestion that, 'since citizens have differing needs, equal treatment requires full account to be taken of their differences'. Moreover, they suggest that society needs to be both cohesive and respectful of diversity: it needs a broadly shared body of values within the national community while respecting deep moral differences between communities within the nation. A vibrant and just society needs, in other words, to recognize and promote both equality and difference. The recognition of difference may, it seems, be necessary in order to realize the very equality that is often expressed in the language of citizenship.

Securing the combination of equality and difference is extremely difficult to achieve in practice. The attempt to recognize difference may lead to fragmentation and a loss of social cohesion, which ultimately undermines equality. For example, the disturbances in Burnley, Oldham and Bradford in the summer of 2001 (Figure 4.1), which were widely reported as 'race riots', led to the creation of both a Ministerial Group on Public Order and Community Cohesion and a Review Team. The Ministerial Group was directed to examine and consider how national policies might be used to promote better community cohesion, based upon shared values *and* a celebration of diversity. The Review Team, led by Ted Cantle, was established to contact local residents and community leaders in the affected towns in order to seek their views on good practice in the handling of these issues at local level (Burnley has a population of about 92,000, including 6000 people from ethnic minorities, mainly Muslim Pakistanis and Bangladeshis). The Cantle Report (Cantle, 2001) argued that the riots in the north of England were caused by the English and Asian communities failing to mix: growing segregation of

FIGURE 4.1   Inter-racial violence in Burnley: Sunday night, 24 June 2001

housing, schooling and employment brought about a deterioration of any sense of social cohesion. Difference, it implied, was institutionalized to the detriment of social cohesion. This anxiety about the loss of social cohesion fuels a widely held sense that equal citizenship presupposes a prior sense of national community with specific shared cultural traditions.

In an attempt to get the balance right, to embrace the cultural and ethnic diversity of British citizens while securing a strong sense of social cohesion among them, the Government (as represented by David Blunkett) suggested in the White Paper on immigration, nationality and asylum entitled *Secure Borders, Safe Haven* (7 February 2002) that two features should unite all British citizens. The first is the English language, which – the paper recommended – should be a mandatory condition for receiving British citizenship; and the second is the values embodied in the European Human Rights Convention, which was adopted as UK law in 1998 (see Figure 4.2). The proposals in this White Paper (which included plans for compulsory citizenship tests and the introduction of a ceremony with a new loyalty oath in which new citizens will be asked to uphold the democratic process as well as swearing allegiance to the Queen, her heirs and successors) were adopted in The Nationality, Immigration and Asylum Act, which received Royal Assent on 7 November 2002.

In addition, and in response to the diverse demands of the current identity politics agenda, the EU issued a directive requiring member states to promote equality in relation to sexual orientation, age and religion in addition to race, gender and disability. Following this, the government announced in May 2002 that it intended to abolish the separate commissions for racial equality, disability rights and women's opportunities, and replace them with one

FIGURE 4.2   Thumbs up to this British citizen enjoying his rights and freedoms (*Independent on Sunday*, 10 February 2002)

equalities body. There was a period of consultation, and then in November 2003 the government announced plans to establish a Commission for Equality and Human Rights, which would promote equal opportunities for all and tackle barriers to participation for all social groups. Significantly, the consultation document itself is called *Equality and Diversity: Making it Happen*, reflecting the extent to which, within contemporary Britain, the pursuit of equality has come to entail a combined recognition of diversity.

There are also changes being introduced in relation to the way in which women (but not minority ethnic groups) are represented within parliament. There are currently 17.9 per cent women MPs in Westminster (see Table 4.1). The Sex Discrimination (Election Candidates) Act 2001 allows for adoption of positive strategies to increase the representation of women in the UK, should political parties choose to adopt such strategies. Between 1993 and 1996, Labour adopted candidate quotas in the form of 'all women short-lists', in which only women would be short-listed for half of the party's 'inheritor' seats and half of its 'challenger' seats. The policy was a controversial one and generated some opposition at a grassroots level. It was dropped in January 1996, following legal challenges brought by two aggrieved male aspirants at an Industrial Tribunal held in Leeds. However, the Sex Discrimination (Election Candidates) Act allows for the re-introduction of gender quotas. Whether or not the parties choose to pursue this option will depend in part upon the ethos and ideology of the parties, but the passing of the act does show that the citizenship practices in Britain are in a period of transition – with a public recognition of difference being introduced into existing equality legislation.

The nature of British citizenship participation is, therefore, slowly changing. Meanwhile, the criteria for citizenship access are also being rethought. In an attempt to establish a 'sense of belonging' to the British nation as a precondition for gaining formal British citizenship, David Blunkett, the current Home Secretary, argues that a 'robust nationality and asylum system' is a precondition of 'our need to be secure within our sense of belonging and identity' (Blunkett, 2002, p.4). The construction of 'secure borders' is proposed as a way of defending the British nation against the destructive effects of globalization and people's increasingly diverse identifications. The White Paper argued that in a world of multiple citizenships 'the country of main residence can and should expect every individual to be committed to accept their responsibilities as well as embracing the rights which citizenship confers' (Blunkett, 2002, p.30).

Recent British citizenship practices indicate that the presumed liberal commitment to formal equality in the public sphere, complemented by diversity within a private sphere, is under development, as marginalized groups demand specific 'rights' to ensure their full and active participation within the public sphere. At the same time, the importance of citizens' responsibilities and cultural belonging is being actively asserted.

TABLE 4.1   Women in West European national parliaments

Rank	Country	Lower or Single House				Upper House or Senate			
		Date of election	Seats[1] (total number)	Seats held by women (number)	Seats held by women (%)	Date of election	Seats[1] (total number)	Seats held by women (number)	Seats held by women (%)
2	Sweden	Sept 2002	349	158	45.3	—	—	—	—
3	Denmark	Nov 2001	179	68	38.0	—	—	—	—
4	Finland	Mar 2003	200	75	37.5	—	—	—	—
6	Norway	Sept 2001	165	60	36.4	—	—	—	—
8	Belgium	May 2003	150	53	35.3	May 2003	71	23	32.4
13	Iceland	May 2003	63	19	30.2	—	—	—	—
49	UK	June 2001	659	118	17.9	n/a	713	117	16.4
65	France	June 2002	574	70	12.2	Sept 2001	321	35	10.9

The data show, in descending order, the number and percentage of women with seats in national parliaments as at 30 October 2003. The West European data have been extracted from world rankings

[1]Figures correspond to the number of seats currently held in parliament

Source: adapted from 'World classification' table, www.ipu.org/wmn-e/classif.htm (accessed 8 January 2004)

3.2 Citizenship in France

French citizenship practices have traditionally been understood as an example of republicanism. The republican tradition stresses the necessity for the state and its citizens to be a community. It places a strong emphasis on the responsibilities of citizens and the need for the integration of the community, leading to a notion of active citizenship 'from below'.

French republicanism was inspired by the classical ideals of the city-state as well as by the ideas of the Enlightenment: fraternity, as well as liberty and equality. This republicanism avoids the liberal language of abstract individualism and is resistant to intermediary voluntary associations in civil society. The state is the expression of society and the organizer of solidarity. French citizenship practices are often understood to draw from Rousseau's *Social Contract* (first published in 1762), which attempts to resolve the apparent tension between being subject to government (which is necessary for security) and retaining one's freedom (which is a moral right) under the notion of the 'general will'. 'Each one of us puts into the community his person and all his powers under the supreme direction of the general will; and as a body, we incorporate every member as an indivisible part of the whole' (Rousseau, 1968, Section I.6).

From this perspective, the state, comprised of its citizens, operates as an organic whole. Influenced by this tradition, French citizenship appears to embody a type of universalism that creates a radical conception of political equality among citizens and at the same time establishes a direct link between the individual and the state. This approach requires the destruction of institutions that come between the individual and the state.

French citizenship practices are, then, usually understood as prime examples of this republican model. For instance, France is a country of immigration. Large immigrant groups of North Africans and Poles arrived just before the First World War. The arrival of Italians between the two world wars was followed by immigrations from the Iberian Peninsula, starting in the 1950s, and from North Africa, starting in the 1960s. However, the official census classifies the population under three categories: French by birth, French by 'acquisition', and foreign. Once foreigners are naturalized, their children born on French soil are declared French by birth. The national and ethnic origin of citizens does not appear in official documents and has no legal status or statistical significance. Moreover, naturalized citizens have been expected to assimilate into the dominant culture, losing – rather than retaining or celebrating – their particular cultural practices. This assimilatory approach to cultural diversity has long been held to be paradigmatically French, arising directly from the French model of republican citizenship.

One consequence of this tradition is the strong opposition to multiculturalism in France compared with that in Britain. In France, multiculturalism is opposed across the political spectrum due to its perceived incompatibility with a conception of 'universal' citizenship, one which demands that all 'particular' identities, such as those of race, ethnicity and gender, which promote part of the republic against the good of the whole, be confined to private life.

Yet this assertion of republican universalism should not be taken to imply that all French citizens have actually had equal legal and political status. For instance, the claim of egalitarian universalism is tempered by the fact that, while universal suffrage gave men formal political rights in 1848, women were not allowed to vote until 1944. Differentiated citizenship is thus an issue not only for ethnic minorities, but also for women. Although the new Constitution of France's Fourth Republic included references to women's equal rights, it was not until François Mitterrand's presidency (1981–95) that a strong public discourse about state feminism and gender equality emerged. Moreover, at the June 1997 general election women still represented only six per cent of the members of the French national parliament. The universal political culture of France has been hostile to women's representation in politics (Siim, 2000, p.63) and, although the discourse of state feminism attempted to introduce a new vocabulary of gender and democratic citizenship, it failed to integrate women into the political elite. France is currently ranked 65 in the league table for the proportion of women in national parliaments, with women making up only 10.9 per cent of the *Assemblée Nationale* (see Table 4.1 above).

Recognition of women's political under-representation led, in the 1990s, to feminist campaigns for 'parity', the demand for equal numbers of male and female representatives in all political bodies. In 1999 Lionel Jospin's government passed a constitutional amendment which inserted a new clause to this effect and, following this, a new electoral law was passed in May 2000, which regulated the proportion of women candidates in local, regional and European elections. The law, applied for the first time in the March 2001 local elections, provides financial penalties for political parties that do not respect the parity principle, public aid being reduced as soon as the deviation from parity reaches two per cent.

The parity debate sparked heated exchanges and raised profound questions about the differing routes to equality for women in politics. Parity is understood as a way of replacing the false universalism of the traditional French republic with a new gender-differentiated universalism. The argument for parity drew on claims both to equality and to sexual difference. Françoise Gaspard, one of the founders of the campaign for parity, states:

> Women have been collectively excluded from politics because of their sex. It is therefore 'as women' that they should claim to be integrated as equal citizens in the city, all the more so since the political institutions bear witness to a special opposition to women's equal access from political institutions.
>
> (Gaspard, 1994, p.41, translated by Siim, 2002, p.67)

Indeed, parity was defended as a way of transcending the old tension between equality and difference. Yet critics of this strategy voiced concerns about this division of humanity and universal citizenship, questioning whether

FIGURE 4.3   Muslims demonstrate against the banning of religious symbols in French schools, December 2003

women as a group have common interests that can be the basis for representation, and emphasizing the problem that parity creates by under-representing more diverse constituencies, notably ethnic minorities.

Meanwhile, the French state has made a determined effort to move away from its assimilatory label in relation to cultural diversity and to embrace a strategy of integration, which allows for a more public affirmation of respect for cultural differences. In November 1989 a public debate about whether Muslim schoolgirls had the right to wear headscarves (the hijab) to (secular) state schools triggered an intense battle about the compatibility of Islam with French secularism. As a result of this debate, all ostentatious religious symbols were banned in educational establishments (Figure 4.3 illustrates the ongoing struggle to retain religious symbols in schools). Yet, shortly after this in 1994, the French state officially recognized the Council of Muslims of France, and Minister Pasqua declared: 'I have always wanted Islam to go from the status of a tolerated religion in France to that of a religion accepted by everyone as part of the French spiritual landscape.' This signalled a shift towards the institutionalized recognition of Islamic groups within the French state.

Following this, integration – not assimilation – became the aim of a whole range of state-funded associations created to facilitate the integration of immigrants into French society. The Ministry for the City, created in 1991, is now called the Ministry for Integration and the Struggle Against Exclusion. This change in official vocabulary may mark an institutional response to demands for a more differentiated citizenship by minority groups, but it may also represent a feeling on the part of the elite that certain, non-European, immigrant groups are inassimilable.

What is clear is that the traditional French rhetoric, whereby the principle of universalism is used to object to all identity differentiation, is now increasingly contradicted by actual state policies. A pragmatic awareness by the French state of the dangers of attempting to repress demands of groups structured on the basis of identity had resulted in the development and subsidy of immigrant 'associations', led by a new breed of cultural intermediaries who negotiate with the public authorities on behalf of the minority communities. This strategy has caused concern among those who fear fragmentation and tribalism: 'the existence of an ethnic market, like any market, makes the agents compete for identity or culture on one hand and the financial resources to promote it on the other' (Kastoryano, 2002, p.105).

Jean-Marie Le Pen, leader of the *Front Nationale*, maintains that there is an indissoluble link between nationality, citizenship and identity. Le Pen laments the fact that citizenship is 'granted too easily' and pleads for a citizenship that is 'inherited and earned'. He clearly speaks for a significant number of French citizens: in the 2002 presidential elections he caused consternation by coming second in the first ballot, eliminating the socialist candidate. Immigration, integration and the negotiation of a common citizenship clearly continue to be perceived as politically charged issues.

We can see from this brief account of citizenship practices in France that the republican tradition is widely held to shape the principles, rhetoric and institutions that characterize the French state's response to the demands of difference. However, we can also see that pragmatic compromise and competing traditions (notably patriarchy) have also had a significant impact, rendering the citizenship practices of contemporary France far more complex than the republican model alone would imply.

3.3 Citizenship in the Nordic countries

The citizenship practices of the Nordic countries (Denmark, Sweden, Norway, Finland and Iceland) are frequently characterized as participatory models of citizenship, based on universalist social policies directed towards all citizens. Danish democracy, for instance, was established in 1849 with the adoption of a free constitution inspired by the French Revolution, which marked a radical but peaceful break with the old monarchy. This constitution gave the vote to all citizens 'except women, undeserving poor, servants, criminals and people who are insane' (Koch and Hvidt, 1999, p.40). Women gained the right to vote in 1915 without the violent suffrage campaigns that occurred in Britain. Since the 1960s women have been active in politics throughout the Nordic countries: 'women are by now fully integrated in all main walks of public decision-making, even if not to an equal extent' (Karvonen and Selle, 1995, p.21).

The presence of women in political institutions has increased dramatically in all the Nordic countries since the 1970s. These countries (with the exception

FIGURE 4.4   *Left:* women Rwandese parliamentarians, 2004: following its 2003 parliamentary elections, Rwanda achieved the highest level of women's representation in the world (almost 49 per cent of members); *right:* women MPs in the Riksdag, Sweden, 2003: as a result of the 2002 elections, women comprised 45 per cent of the members in the Swedish Parliament

of Iceland) had the highest levels of women's representation in the world until the 2003 elections, which placed Rwanda ahead of Sweden in world rankings (from which the data in Table 4.1 above has been extracted; see also Figure 4.4). Women's political mobilization has had a profound affect on the political culture in Denmark. Gender equality in politics became an official political goal. Both the Social Democratic Party and the Socialist People's Party adopted party quotas for internal elections in the party, and later adopted candidate quotas for elections to parliament. Interestingly, the parties later abandoned these quotas, following the proposal that they do so from young female party members. Nonetheless, the number of women representatives to parliament has continued to grow, indicating that formal rules have had only limited effect. Comparative research within the Nordic countries reveals the Danish route to women's increased participation to be distinct from that experienced in Sweden and Norway, being based primarily on women's organization 'from below' rather than their integration into political parties.

Women's political and social citizenship has differed markedly between the Nordic countries and France. These differences have shaped and defined recent attempts to gain greater access to full citizenship participation by women. As Siim points out, 'the idea of parity of women and men in political bodies [in France] has different philosophical roots and different practical implications from the quota system practices in the Nordic countries' (Siim, 2000, p.69). Parity, as adopted in France, focuses on 'biological difference', while the Nordic quota system focuses on women's historical marginality to politics. The demand for parity is a demand for a permanent right: the demand for quotas is understood as a transitory measure needed to integrate minority groups. Parity privileges a legal strategy, while quotas in the Nordic countries have been the result of political processes. Significantly, parity is a principle rooted in the universalist political culture of the French Republic. In contrast, quota systems engage with the participatory discourses of Nordic citizenship and are more amenable to demands for a multi-differentiated citizenship. In other words, different political systems respond to the demands of difference and equality, or the tensions between common citizenship and plural identities, in quite distinct ways.

3.4 Citizenship in Belgium

Belgium is bi-cultural and multinational, characterized by linguistic conflict between the Flemings and Walloons. Belgium works with a 'consociational' model of citizenship, in which executive power and economic resources are distributed in proportion to the size of the different linguistic communities that comprise the polity. People in the northern part of Belgium, Flanders, speak Flemish (Dutch); those in the southern part, Wallonia, speak French. The formal equality of Belgium's two languages was officially recognized in 1898. In 1932, official unilingualism was recognized in Flanders and Wallonia and, in 1993, Belgium was officially transformed into a federal state.

Debates about difference in Belgium have not, therefore, focused on race relations and racism, as they have in the UK: racism has not been seen as an internal Belgian issue. Rather, linguistic and territorial issues have dominated public discourses and institutional arrangements. This is perhaps one of the clearest examples of a separatist model of citizenship we can find in practice. The state operates on the basis that each linguistic community remains separate from others. As Belgian political scientist Dirk Jacobs notes, Belgium 'always has a very intolerant political culture, distrustful of other communities and limiting itself to rigid pillarization and political patronage' (Jacobs, 2002, p.123).

Belgium's separatist citizenship practices institutionalize linguistic differences as absolute, while allowing no space for other sorts of differences to be recognized institutionally or culturally. For example, following Belgium's colonial period, former Belgian subjects (from the Congo, Rwanda and Burundi) were refused Belgian citizenship: 'black subjects were not allowed to become a part of the Belgian nation' (Jacobs, 2002, p.132). The whole issue of ethnic diversity has not, therefore, gained the central place within citizenship practices that it has in the UK.

Gender difference, however, has been addressed within the Belgian political system. Belgium currently has 35.3 per cent representation of women in the lower house and 32.4 per cent in the upper house (see Table 4.1). A legal framework stipulates that electoral lists may contain a maximum of two-thirds of candidates of the same sex. This law was first applied during the European, federal and regional elections of June 1999 and there have since been attempts in both houses to strengthen this quota. In other words Belgium, with its separatist citizenship practices, has opted for legally imposed gender quotas. This stands in contrast to the informal party-based quotas adopted in the Nordic countries and now being introduced in the UK, and also to France's adoption of parity legislation. Like France, it has opted for a constitutional solution. Yet, as in the UK, Belgium must reconcile this institutional recognition of difference with other differences (here linguistic). Compare, for example, the significance of class in Westminster and language in Belgium. Each of these democratic systems institutionalizes the political significance of certain differences, while excluding others from political view.

SUMMARY

In order to explore the complexity of the different outcomes, it is pertinent to examine the nationality laws – who may become a citizen and who may not – and the nature of citizenship as reflected in citizenship practices. This can be seen in relation to the issues of minority ethnic groups and gender, in the citizenship practices in Britain, France, the Nordic countries and Belgium.

Features of the British model:

- British citizenship has traditionally been hierarchical in nature and taken the form of 'subjects with rights'.

- The conditions of contemporary multiculturalism have promoted new thinking on citizenship which lays greater emphasis on the articulation of difference.

- Precisely how this will be integrated with continuing principles of equality remains a major topic of debate and has yet to be resolved.

Features of the French model:

- It is set within a republican tradition which stresses the need for community integration.

- The stress on assimilation has marginalized multicultural practices, while largely ignoring women's participation.

- New emphases on parity and inclusion have now modified the traditional republican policies of promoting a largely formal equality.

Features of the Nordic model:

- Women have been particularly strongly integrated into the political life of Nordic countries.

- This has been achieved more through the use of quota systems than through policies based on the parity principle applied in France, thus illustrating different responses to citizenship demands in these countries.

Features of the Belgian model:

- The key differences prominent in Belgian citizenship debates have not concerned race but the indigenous language groups.

- Demands for equality and the recognition of difference have here been reconciled through separatist policies and the establishment of a federal state.

4 COMPARING CITIZENSHIP MODELS

It is important to adopt a contextual and comparative approach to citizenship studies. Without this, as French political scientist Riva Kastoryano warns, one generates studies 'guided more by ideological reconstructions than by present realities, more by concepts that have made the history of ideas than by facts that have shaped history' (Kastoryano, 2002, p.40). Yet, it is also helpful to have a clear understanding of the conceptual issues at stake.

We have seen that citizenship defines the relationship between the individual and the state. It generates both rights and duties. The precise nature of these rights and duties varies with different citizenship models. Citizenship rights traditionally comprise civil, political and social rights, while citizenship duties traditionally entail assimilation into a nation or integration into a state. Within this, there are various possible theoretical models of citizenship. Four central theoretical models of citizenship are the liberal, republican, participatory and consociational (Box 4.2). The present realities of citizenship are frequently complex and fluid, such that actual citizenship practices rarely map neatly and directly on to these models, but the models are useful nonetheless for understanding and evaluating diverse citizenship practices.

BOX 4.2	**Four possible citizenship models**

Liberal

There is a single political culture in the public sphere but substantial diversity in the private lives of individuals and communities.

Republican

The state promotes a single national culture and expects all to assimilate to it. People who do not or cannot assimilate are second-class citizens.

Participatory

There is both unity and diversity in public life; communities and identities overlap and are interdependent, and develop common features.

Consociational

The state permits and expects each community to remain separate from others and to organize and regulate its own affairs. The state largely confines itself to maintaining order and civility.

Each of the models of citizenship aims to secure equality for all citizens, though this equality is understood in quite diverse ways: from the minimal equality of civil rights, to the more substantive equality of social and cultural responsibilities. The liberal model of citizenship, for instance, aims to make differences of identities politically irrelevant, while the consociational model of citizenship entrenches these differences within political institutions.

The liberal model of citizenship, conceived as a set of rights enjoyed equally by each member of the society in question, embodies an idea of social justice. There is a common set of political entitlements whatever the social, cultural and economic status of the individual. The primary focus of concern tends to be the relation between citizenship and economic inequality, requiring a minimum level of redistribution to overcome the pressures of social exclusion. Citizenship is conceived as a political identity working to mitigate other (primarily economic) identities (see the writings of American political theorist John Rawls for one of the strongest articulations of this citizenship model). For Rawls, citizenship is a public political status taking precedence over private personal identities in that the pursuit of the latter can only take place within the boundaries set by the former. Advocates of this model assume that, while people's personal identities may be deeply entrenched or 'encumbered', as citizens they 'claim the right to view their persons as independent from and as not identified with any particular conception of the good, or scheme of private ends' (Rawls, 1985, p.241). Citizenship, here, focuses on formal equality before the law, in order to create a society in which one is free to pursue one's own life as one thinks best (as long as this pursuit does not infringe upon another's right to do the same). Diversity is thus safeguarded in the private sphere through the uniform application of rules in the public sphere.

The republican model of citizenship, in contrast, 'conceives the citizen as someone who plays an active role in shaping the future direction of his or her society through political debate and decision-making' (Miller, 2000, p.114). It augments the liberal conception of citizenship as rights with an added correlative stress on responsibilities, specifically a responsibility to promote the common good of the political community through active participation in its political life. Reacting against the perceived individualism and passivity of the liberal model, the republican tradition emphasizes an active, collective politics as the essence of citizenship. Where the liberal conception of citizenship is overtly based upon pluralism, the republican one more directly presumes the common traditions and heritage of a culturally homogenous society. It aspires to a substantive rather than a formal conception of citizenship, jettisoning the liberal attempt to distinguish the right from the good.

There are clearly problems attendant upon adopting either of these conceptions of citizenship. If, for example, one defines citizenship narrowly in relation to formal rights (as liberals tend to do) one is open to the charge of failing to understand the importance of national culture, tradition, heritage and 'the ties that bind' citizens together through a shared sense of collective identity, which goes beyond a formal legal relation to a state. This is because if the state acts as a neutral arbiter between competing demands and citizens are required only to abide by minimal laws, then the necessary basis to ensure social cohesion, which is generated by a common national culture, may be absent. The models may tend to privilege diversity at the expense of cohesion.

If, on the other hand, one defines citizenship extensively (as republicans do) one becomes open to the charge that the polity is overly assimilatory, demanding too high a degree of conformity of its citizens; it will present a single model of the active citizen, one which is actually partial and therefore substantively exclusionary. The republican model of citizenship entails the state having a duty to ensure that everyone assimilates to the dominant national culture. Citizens will have a responsibility to cultivate shared loyalties. Accordingly, the potential weakness of this model is that it may privilege cohesion at the expense of diversity.

The more fleshed-out the conception of the citizenship, the more likely it is that many will feel themselves to be 'second-class citizens', granted formal rights of residence, but not meeting the more extensive criteria of inclusion. Norman Tebbitt's famous 'cricket test', which encouraged immigrant communities to show the degree of their assimilation by supporting British sporting teams, provides a good example of this. (In April 1990, Tebbitt, then a Conservative MP, told the *Los Angeles Times* that it would be 'an interesting test' to see how many British Asian immigrants cheered on the teams of their country of origin rather than England at cricket.) Citizenship can become an overly moralized discourse used to discipline a recalcitrant population into cultural conformity.

The participatory model, situated midway between the liberal and republican models, accepts the need for a social cohesion which is stronger than that offered by the liberal model, but weaker than that demanded by the republican model. The participatory model aims to cultivate a shared *political* culture in the public sphere which will allow for diversity in the social and cultural relations of the private sphere, but many are sceptical about the feasibility of these twin commitments. If, for example, the political culture is one that positively affirms gender equality (as has been the case in the Nordic countries), this may actively work against the toleration of ethnic minorities which are deemed to perpetuate cultural practices based on strictly divergent gender roles.

Finally, our fourth model of citizenship, the consociational model, offers a vision of separate, rather than overlapping, communities within a state. Here, the duty of the state is to protect the distinct communities within its boundaries, and the primary loyalty of citizens is to their community. The problem is that this model can institutionalize and rigidify what were fairly fluid differences and affiliations, making certain identities the basis of one's access to political power and therefore entrenching them both politically and culturally. This can result in an increasing inability of people to identify and understand others across group boundaries, leading to a fragmentation of the polity.

While these models of citizenship are analytically distinct, most citizenship practices invoke various combinations of the models, and many political theorists recommend a critical synthesis of various elements within the models. Some critics argue that while formal civil and political rights inscribe the liberal conception of citizenship, more substantive social and economic rights would actually help realize the republican conception of citizenship by creating the conditions for full social and political participation (Lister, 1997). Such a resolution usually focuses on the fact that while the formal civil and political rights clearly inscribe the liberal conception of citizenship, the more substantive social and economic rights actually help realize the republican conception of citizenship by creating the conditions for full social and political participation. Radical democrats make appeal to republicanism, stressing the importance of political participation and substantive social and economic inclusion, while more conservative forms of contemporary communitarianism adopt similar discourses of social inclusion to focus instead upon social obligation and the importance of cultural assimilation. In the face of these assimilatory tendencies within republican citizenship discourses, many ethnic groups have found the liberal citizenship discourse rather more appealing.

It has become increasingly clear, however, that to think of citizenship from the standpoint of particular group identities is to challenge the assumption of traditional citizenship rhetoric. The very factors that propel such a wide range of theorists to make appeal to 'citizenship' as a common status which might provide a framework for a just and peaceful co-existence, also seem to expose citizenship as an impossible and even oppressive discourse. The simultaneous desirability and impossibility of the neutral state and universal citizenship is a paradox that increasingly haunts these debates.

The antagonism between demands for equality and difference frequently appear intractable in theory. Hall suggests that the tension may not be amenable to resolution in the abstract, but maintains that 'it can be negotiated in practice' (Hall, 2002, p.235). A brief survey of the citizenship practices of various European states reveals that different pragmatic solutions are being pursued within the context of political discourse and institutions, which have been framed by different models of citizenship, but which are not entirely circumscribed by them.

SUMMARY

- Four distinctive citizenship models can be identified: liberal, republican, participatory and consociational.
- Each model attempts to reconcile the conflicting demands for equality and difference in a particular way, although a fully satisfying resolution within a single theory may be ultimately unattainable.

5 MAPPING CITIZENSHIP PRACTICES ON TO MODELS

A contextual and comparative approach to citizenship reveals that different states invoke different citizenship practices (discussed in Section 3), which sometimes – but not always – map on to the models of citizenship developed by critics and theorists (discussed in Section 4).

Britain, France, the Nordic countries and Belgium have traditionally adopted citizenship practices that map fairly closely on to the liberal, republican, participatory and consociational models of citizenship, respectively. British citizenship, for example, has been characterized as 'passive', with a strong emphasis on private liberty, premised on a strict division between the public and private spheres; it is therefore viewed as a clear example of a liberal form of citizenship. France, in contrast, where citizenship is associated with the struggle for political, but not social, rights, is most often understood to operate with a republican form of citizenship. Meanwhile, Nordic citizenship combines active participatory citizenship with universal social rights. It has been described as a mix of these two traditions, idealizing neither the state, as in the French case, nor the private sphere, as in the British case. Finally, the Belgian system is frequently understood as a form of consociational citizenship.

However, political systems are complex, dynamic and often contradictory: they never conform absolutely to theoretical models. For example, the fact that France is witnessing the emergence of 'cultural intermediaries', who negotiate with the public authorities on behalf of minority communities, indicates that it is departing from a strict republican model of citizenship in certain respects in an attempt to respond to the political pressures posed by some ethnic minorities. The British Nationality, Immigration and Asylum Act 2002 now requires those seeking naturalization to swear loyalty to the British nation, learn the English language and develop a sense of belonging to a British culture (as we noted earlier), which suggests that it too is departing from a strict liberal model of citizenship in these respects in an attempt to respond to the political pressures posed by certain aspects of migration.

Nonetheless, the ways in which the countries under consideration here have attempted to facilitate the active participation of citizens in their polities have clearly been shaped by the dominant citizenship practices that prevail. We can see this if we look at the issue of the political participation of women within these countries. The Nordic countries have a culture that has been characterized by the active participation of women in all areas of public decision making, including politics. The Nordic political parties, in keeping with a participatory model of citizenship, were among the very first to use quotas to encourage the active participation of women in the political process.

Britain, with much lower levels of women MPs, has only recently passed legislation on this issue and, in keeping with a liberal model of citizenship, it is *permissive* rather than mandatory – allowing political parties to introduce positive strategies to increase the number of female candidates they field only if they choose to do so.

France, with extremely low levels of female participation in party politics until very recently, opted for a constitutional amendment to regulate the proportion of women candidates. This was not a transitory measure to address women's political marginalization (as was the case in the Nordic countries and more recently in the British Labour Party), but a legal strategy rooted in the universalist culture of French republicanism. Belgium, which has also opted for a constitutional solution, differs from France in that it perceives the political representation of women to be an issue to be negotiated alongside other issues of diversity, notably the representation of linguistic communities (while advocates of parity legislation in France steadfastly maintained that its introduction had no implications at all with regard to minority ethnic representation).

From a brief survey of these indicators, we can see that the tension between common citizenship and plural identities is currently being negotiated by each of these modern democracies, but it is being negotiated in different ways by different governments, according to the dominant citizenship practices. The Nordic countries have been largely assimilatory and unable to affirm publicly ethnic and religious differences within their citizenship practices. Similarly, France has been more resistant to the demands of difference than Belgium has, yet even France introduced parity legislation. Britain has tended to adopt integrationist rather than assimilatory policies regarding ethnic and religious difference, so is potentially open to multicultural demands. However, the dominance of class in shaping the existing party system works as a clear barrier to the institutional recognition of more plural differences.

We can see, then, that even among the liberal democratic states within Europe there are widely divergent responses and policies to the demand that citizenship practices entail the participation of currently marginalized groups.

SUMMARY

- The four citizenship models broadly underlie the different citizenship practices seen in Britain, France, Belgium and the Nordic countries.
- Most have been subject to recent change in response to the various demands of minority ethnic groups and attempts to counteract the political exclusion of women.
- Even these contemporary changes have been approached and negotiated in ways that reflect established citizenship practices.

6   CONCLUSION: NEW FORMS OF CITIZENSHIP?

Socio-economic changes within modern democratic states in Western Europe have worked to erode the significance of certain differences and magnify the significance of others. The perceived importance of class has dwindled within public and political debates. At the same time, gender, ethnicity, sexuality, age, disability and national identity have all gained increasing political salience. This has had a profound effect on political culture (though a lesser effect on the political institutions as yet). There has been a move to pluralize the differences deemed to be politically significant. There is also a determination among many minority groups to shift the focus of political attention away from eradicating difference (understood as economy inequality) towards recognizing differences (of cultural identity). This requires the relation between equality and difference to be rethought.

On the one hand, marginalized groups demand greater equality. On the other hand, they demand greater public affirmation of their legitimate differences. Another significant manifestation of a politics of difference takes the form of demands for devolution and self-determination. These demands are motivated by a concern with national identity. They issue a challenge to the legitimacy of the state and attempt to redefine the territorial scope of citizenship. Each of these assertions of difference – gendered, ethnic, national – challenges existing understandings of the nature and boundary of the political. Together, they have focused attention on a broader understanding of politics, which extends into civil society and the domestic sphere. They have also questioned the representativeness of modern democratic institutions.

Different citizenship models respond to the demands of difference within the polity in distinct ways. The demands of feminism and multiculturalism, for instance, have been felt by states that have liberal, republican, participatory and consociational forms of citizenship. Accordingly, as Hall points out, just as there are different multicultural societies, so there are different multiculturalisms (Hall, 2002, p.210).

Conservative multiculturalism insists on the assimilation of difference into the traditions and customs of the majority (and is compatible with a republican model of citizenship). Liberal multiculturalism seeks to integrate the different cultural groups as fast as possible into the 'mainstream' provided by a universal individual citizenship, tolerating only in private any particular cultural practices. Pluralist multiculturalism (consistent with a consociational model of citizenship) formally enfranchises the differences among groups along cultural lines and accords different group rights to different communities within a more communal and communitarian political order. The participatory form of citizenship in the Nordic countries, which has done so much to pursue gender equality, has – surprisingly – done little as yet to engage with the challenges posed by participation for minority ethnic citizenship.

Overall, the demands of difference have challenged the 'false universalism' of traditional citizenship models, in all their diverse forms. However, these demands have not culminated in the abandoning of citizenship as a universalist goal. As Lister suggests: 'Instead we can aspire to a universalism that stands in creative tension to diversity and difference' (Lister, 1997, p.66). The challenge is to negotiate such a differentiated universalism.

This makes the issue of identity central to current debates about citizenship, and such identity politics has frequently been used to justify an endorsement of group representation. For instance, Iris Marion Young, in her book *Justice and the Politics of Difference* (1990), suggests that attachment to specific traditions, practices, language and other culturally specific forms is a crucial aspect of social existence. Groups that have suffered oppression need guaranteed representation in order that their distinct voice can be heard. A just polity, she argues, requires the participation and inclusion of all groups, which is only secured by differential treatment for oppressed groups (Young, 1990, p.184).

Liberal critics of this endorsement tend to assume that the practice of granting group rights, including representation rights, will inevitably strengthen an idea of identity as given, or essential, which works to the detriment of individual autonomy. They express concern at the essentialism implicit in these arguments, suggesting that all advocates of group rights necessarily rely on the idea that members of groups have some sort of primordial attachment to certain cultural practices or social perspectives which need to be sustained.

Moreover, the tendency to focus on strategies of inclusion rather than issues of exclusion frequently neglects the plight of those who still do not have citizenship status. The issue of access to citizenship, discussed at the beginning of this chapter, may – in other words – be marginalized by a focus on the increased participation of existing citizens within the polity. The greater integration into the nation-state of ethnic minorities who already have formal citizenship status may, paradoxically, be achieved at the cost of creating stronger boundaries around the nation-state, which will make it harder for asylum seekers and refugees to gain even formal access.

It is because of these concerns that some people now advocate a multilayered conception of citizenship. Recent technological, economic and political developments have, arguably, made the need for such a multilayered conception of citizenship increasingly important. Others argue that citizenship simply makes no sense beyond the boundaries of a nation-state (Miller, 2000, p.81). A republican model of citizenship, in which the active citizens take part along with others in shaping the future direction of their society through political debate, is a form of bounded citizenship. It is precisely because it is such a rich conception of citizenship, aspiring to a polity in which diverse beliefs and styles of life co-exist under shared laws and institutions which all can endorse as legitimate, that it cannot be sustained beyond a limited community. Could it be that the 'safe haven' of citizenship requires 'secure borders', which work against an open embrace of new citizens, including asylum seekers?

Negotiating the twin commitments to equality and difference within our models of citizenship is a complex process. Modern democracies are dealing with tensions between common citizenship and plural identities in ways that are shaped by their particular citizenship practices. These practices frame citizens' understandings of what citizenship entails, and what the appropriate terms of access and participation should be.

REFERENCES

Alibhai-Brown, Y. (2000) *After Multiculturalism,* Foreign Policy Centre, London.

Blunkett, D. (2002) 'Foreword', *Secure Borders, Safe Haven: Integration with Diversity in Modern Britain*, Home Office, White Paper, Cm 5387.

Brubaker, R. (1992) *Citizenship and Nationhood in France and Germany,* Cambridge, MA, Harvard University Press.

Cantle, T. (2001) *Community Cohesion: A Report of the Independent Review Team*, Home Office, http://www.homeoffice.gov.uk/docs2/comm_cohesion.html (accessed 11 February 2004).

Etzioni, A. (1993) *The Spirit of Community*, New York, Touchstone.

Gaspard, F. (1994) 'De la parite: genese d'un concept, naissance d'un Mouvement', *Nouvelle Questions Feministes,* vol.15, no.4, pp.29–44.

Hall, S. (1993) 'Culture, community, nation', *Cultural Studies*, vol.7, no.3, pp.349–63.

Hall, S. (2002) 'Conclusion: the multi-cultural question' in Hesse, B. (ed.) *Un/settled Multiculturalism*, London, Zed Books.

Jacobs, D. (2002) 'Giving foreigners the vote: ethnocentrism in Dutch and Belgian political debates' in ter Wal, J. and Verkuyten, M. (eds) *Comparative Perspectives on Racism*, Aldershot, Ashgate.

Karvonen, L. and Selle, P. (eds) (1995) *Women in Nordic Politics: Closing the Gap*, Aldershot, Dartmouth.

Kastoryano, R. (2002) *Negotiating Identities: States and Immigrants in France and Germany*, Oxford, Princeton University Press.

Koch, H. and Kvidt, K. (1999) *The Danish Constitutions*, Copenhagen, Christian Eilerts Forlag.

Lister, R. (1997) *Citizenship: Feminist Perspectives*, Basingstoke, Macmillan.

Marshall, T.H. (1950) *Citizenship and Social Class*, Cambridge, Cambridge University Press.

Miller, D. (2000) *Citizenship and National Identity*, Cambridge, Polity Press.

Parekh, B. (2000) *The Future of Multi-Ethnic Britain*, London, Profile Books.

Rawls, J. (1985) 'Justice as fairness: political not metaphysical', *Philosophy and Public Affairs*, vol.14, no.3, pp.223–51.

Rawls, J. (1993) *Political Liberalism*, New York, Columbia University Press.

Rex, J. (1986) *Race and Ethnicity*, Buckingham, Open University Press.

Rousseau, J.-J. (1968) *The Social Contract* (ed. M. Cranston), Harmondsworth, Pengiun, first published in 1762.

Siim, B. (2000) *Gender and Citizenship*, Cambridge, Cambridge University Press.

Soysal, Y. (1994) *Limits of Citizenship: Migrants and Post-national Membership in Europe*, Chicago, IL, University of Chicago Press.

Taylor, C. (1994) 'The politics of recognition' in Gutmann, A. (ed.) *Multiculturalism*, Princeton, NJ, Princeton University Press.

Young, I.M. (1990) *Justice and the Politics of Difference*, Princeton, NJ, Princeton University Press.

FURTHER READING

Heater, D. (1999) *What is Citizenship?*, Cambridge, Polity Press.

Brubaker, R. (1992) *Citizenship and Nationhood in France and Germany*, Cambridge, MA, Harvard University Press.

Siim, B. (2000) *Gender and Citizenship*, Cambridge, Cambridge University Press.

Story telling and theory building: comparing political worlds

Andrew Dobson

Evidence & argument

chapter

Contents

1 INTRODUCTION: COMPARING THINGS, COMPARING WORLDS

This chapter continues our theme of comparing political worlds. It is about why we might want to compare them, what we are comparing, the difficulties of comparison, and strategies for trying to overcome these difficulties. So it examines in more detail how we address the issues first raised by Paul Lewis in the Introduction to this book, issues that have been explored in various contexts in the intervening chapters.

The first thing that probably strikes us when thinking about political worlds is how many of them there are. Just *how* many there are depends, of course, on what we think a political world is. Some might say that individual human beings are political worlds: each of us with our own political understandings and aspirations, each of us both the source and the destination of the exercise of political power. If this is right then there are about six billion political worlds for us to consider. We could talk of some, perhaps unexpected, political worlds, such as a pub and a refugee detention camp – even a supermarket checkout queue (see **Huysmans, 2005**). It's especially important to remember that the 'stateless peoples' such as the Kurds, referred to by Bram Gieben and Paul Lewis in Chapter 2 (Section 3), also inhabit political worlds even though they don't occupy a fixed territory of the type we tend to associate with the nation-state.

Despite all this variety, however, the comparison of political worlds in political science, or what is normally called 'comparative politics', usually takes political worlds to mean 'countries'. This still gives us quite a large number with which to work. There are about 200 independent states in the world today, and all of them are potential candidates for comparative political inquiry (Figure 5.1). Of course, the claim that this is 'quite a large number' is already a comparative claim – 'quite large compared with what?' might be the response. To those who study molecules or tadpoles, 200 is actually a very small number, and I shall return to the significance of such comparisons later on.

More specifically, comparative politics is about comparing aspects of countries' political systems. So, comparativists typically compare and contrast the component parts of political parties and electoral systems, for instance – and even more intangible phenomena such as 'political culture'.

A key question in this chapter is whether, despite their peculiarities, we can build theories for comparing political worlds that will enable us to offer general truths about them. Or are we only ever able to tell stories about them – stories rich in specific detail but devoid of generalizable truths?

FIGURE 5.1   Two types of political world. *Left:* members of the Connecticut House of Representatives, 2004; *right:* highest ranking elders in Masai society, Kenya, 1963

Let's begin with the act of comparison itself, and see what lessons we might draw for the science (or is it an art?) of comparing political systems. Write down a list of ten countries. Any ten will do – you don't have to think too hard about it.

Here are the ten that came to my mind: Venezuela, France, Japan, United States, Angola, Great Britain, Australia, China, Luxembourg, Ghana.

Where did that list come from? Well, personal and professional associations mostly, and a couple of the countries happened to be in the news this morning. The list is not totally random, but more or less so – and certainly I'd give you a different list tomorrow. The point is that any ten countries will do.

There are all sorts of different things you might do with this list, and what you do with it will surely depend on *why* you are doing it. In the beginning of the Introduction, Lewis gave us some good examples of questions that students of comparative politics ask themselves, and why they ask them. Later we shall see what happens if we are comparing for the particular purposes of comparative politics, but here I want to draw out some general characteristics of the act of comparison – the relevance will become clear to you later on. So, someone compiling an index for an atlas, for example, would want to put the names of different countries in alphabetical order. Let's say for a moment, then, that we are indexers. Write down your list of countries in alphabetical order.

Here is my list: Angola, Australia, China, France, Ghana, Great Britain, Japan, Luxembourg, United States, Venezuela.

What is the first thing you notice about your list? The first thing I notice is that it is still a list – just in a different order. This makes it clear that classification is not the same as comparison. So what would happen if someone asked me to *compare* the countries in this list? How would I set about the comparison, and what might such a comparison do to the list? Let's say for the moment that we are carrying out this comparison of the countries only in terms of the alphabetical information we have about them. We need know nothing more about them at all. Think for a moment or two, then, about your list of ten countries and how you would compare them in terms of their alphabetical properties. Write down your new list.

Well, I've just done my list, and it looks exactly the same as my original alphabetical one – with one exception in terms of the way it is organized. When I thought about comparing these countries, I noticed that two of them begin with the letter 'A' and two of them begin with the letter 'G'. In terms of first letters, then, two sets of countries were the *same* as each other (Angola and Australia, and Ghana and Great Britain). Having established this, we can also say that the remaining six countries are *different* from one another and from the rest.

What did your comparative list look like? Maybe none of your countries began with the same letter. Does this make comparison impossible? Not necessarily. You probably found other ways of comparing them in terms of their alphabetical properties. You might, for example, have chosen the *last* letter of each country as the term of comparison. As it happens, five of my countries end with the letter 'a' and two with the letter 'n'. I can then say that two groups of countries are the *same* as each other, one group's countries are *different* from those of the other group, and that three countries are *different* both from one another and from the other seven.

What have we learnt about comparison from this little experiment? Exercises in comparison share common features:

- We begin by *compiling a list of things* to compare. This was our original list of countries. Such a list is sometimes called an undifferentiated list because we haven't looked for a way of sorting out the differences among the things in it.

- *Sorting* involves looking for common features of what's being studied – in our case, countries' names.

- This process of selection enabled us to *classify* the countries into groups – countries whose first letters were 'A' or 'G' for example.

- Finally, we were able to *carry out a basic act of comparison* by saying, for example, that Angola and Australia are the same as each other in that they both begin with the same capital letter, and that this makes them different from Ghana and Great Britain which begin with a different one.

Now that we have some idea of what comparing things involves, we can turn our attention to continuing the business in hand – comparing political worlds.

2 WHY COMPARE POLITICAL WORLDS?

Why might we want to compare political worlds at all? One answer is that comparative political inquiry is an extension of what we do, and seem to need to do, in our everyday lives. Each day most of us find ourselves describing, explaining and predicting *something*. Comparative politics is no more, then, than carrying out these apparently basic human activities in the context of what we are calling 'political worlds'.

But of course this context supplies its own extra and particular reasons for carrying out these more general human activities. First, we do comparative politics in the expectation that it will simplify a complex political reality and make it more manageable. We saw from our indexing experiment that the act of comparison, via classification, has the effect of simplifying long lists. My list of ten countries was reduced to three groups (countries beginning with 'A', beginning with 'G', and beginning with neither 'A' nor 'G'). I don't know what happened to your list, but I suspect something similar occurred. In this sense, comparative politics is like a map. All maps simplify a much more complex reality and help us to find our way around it. Students of comparative politics are therefore map makers, cartographers who help us find our way around multiple and complex political worlds. They try to make sense of the variety Gieben and Lewis refer to in Chapter 2 (Section 2): 'states differ on a number of counts. They may be more or less powerful, large or small, strong or weak, rich or poor, stable or unstable, legitimate or illegitimate'.

Second, comparative politics inevitably brings us into contact with political worlds other than our own. In order to carry out a comparison you need more than one thing. You cannot compare one thing with itself at one particular time – you have to compare it with something else or at least, say, the same country at a different time. Not only do you need a minimum of two things if you want to carry out an act of comparison, but these two things also need to be *different*. You cannot compare two identical things. So, comparative politics brings us into contact with different political worlds. Sometimes the act of comparison is between 'our' home country and another one, or ones. Sometimes it is between countries other than 'our own', and sometimes it is a combination of the two. In each of these cases the comparativist will see that other countries do things differently, and this can have the effect of expanding our political and cultural horizons. If we assume that knowledge of others is a prerequisite for finding our way around, and managing, a globalizing world, then comparative politics seems to be of increasing practical importance.

Third, comparison of countries can also help us test hypotheses about them in a way that might lead us to talk of a science of comparative politics. It enables us to move beyond mere description, towards explanation. We might suspect, for example, that countries with big divides between rich people and poor people are more prone to revolutions than countries with a more equal division of wealth. The hypothesis, then, is that big disparities of wealth lead to revolution. How do we test this hypothesis? It is obviously no good finding just one country where this is true and hoping to draw the conclusion that it is always true. We need to *compare* that country with other ones that have a similar wealth distribution profile to see if the hypothesis continues to hold true. We might find that in one or two cases it does not, leading us to refine our hypothesis ('revolutions occur when disparities of wealth are increasing at a faster rate than wealth is being created', for example). This new hypothesis will lead to further comparative testing, and so on.

Sometimes these hypotheses are tested 'for the thrill of the chase', or to refine the techniques that lead to effective testing. Sometimes, though, comparative politics is done with very practical and particular objectives in mind. Finding out under what conditions revolutions occur, for example, might be regarded as a step on the way to avoiding – or perhaps encouraging – them (Figure 5.2). This would be an instance of another reason for doing comparative politics: the possibility of prediction. The ability to predict is an essential part of getting through everyday life, and policy makers, too, are attracted to the possibility of knowing that under certain social conditions, policy X will produce outcome Y.

FIGURE 5.2 Can comparative politics help us to find our way?

So, just as we find ourselves describing, explaining and predicting a whole range of phenomena in our everyday lives, comparativists try to describe, explain and predict political worlds. To do so, they:

- identify common features of those worlds

- classify them

- search for patterns in them

- reach comparative conclusions.

Their objective, in other words, is to make sense of the complex political reality contained in the two hundred or so independent states that are their objects of study, and they do so by employing the comparative method.

3 FACTS AND VALUES IN THE COMPARATIVE METHOD

We have begun to consider how and why researchers engage in the comparative method. But what is the status of this method? What kind of enquiry is it? How can we know whether the researcher has indeed 'made sense' of the political worlds being compared? In particular, can we be sure that the researcher is not 'contaminating' the comparison by bringing their own values to it?

Look for a moment at Box 5.1.

BOX 5.1

Many people coming to research for the first time have a tendency to think that they are in the business of establishing 'the truth' about a particular issue or subject. They want to find out 'the facts', or want to 'prove' (or perhaps disprove) a particular argument. They believe that they can be 'objective' in their research, and that others will sit up and take notice when they present their findings.

(Baxter *et al.*, 2001, p.14)

How do you react to this, both as someone who might undertake comparative research on political worlds, and as someone who might hope to learn from such research?

Presumably, both the researcher and the student would want truth rather than lies, fact rather than fiction, and objective knowledge rather than knowledge serving a particular end or point of view. This is what we usually mean when we talk of 'making sense' of something. So when the comparativist concludes that countries with proportional systems, such as the German AMS system discussed by Mark Smith in Chapter 3 (Section 5), are more likely to have coalition governments than those that have an SMPS (the UK, for example), we assume that this is the truth, that it has not been made up, and that the conclusion has been reached independently of any beliefs the researcher may have about proportional representation. What we want is evidence rather than unsupported argument.

By the same token, imagine yourself as a 'producer' rather than as a 'consumer' of comparative politics research. You are intent on examining the hypothesis, say, that countries with weak trade unions show higher economic growth rates than those with strong trade unions. The objective, presumably, is to reach conclusions about this that people will have reason to believe. Two of the criteria that people will use to assess the credibility of your research are: first, you have dealt only with facts; and, second, you have no stake in the conclusions reached. If you are not persuaded of this, then consider what your own reaction to this research might be upon discovering that it has been carried out by a trade unionist or, alternatively, by the managing director of a big company, such as ICI or Shell. It is a natural instinct to think of 'bias' rather than 'truth' as a possibility in these circumstances.

Are we perhaps considering a rather special case? Trade unionists and managing directors might each have a political point to make, but surely political scientists have no stake in the research they undertake and the conclusions they reach? Their aim is not to make a political point but to produce credible research and – as we saw above – the currency of credibility is the facts, and the criterion of credibility is the truth. The stake that comparativists have in their work is therefore internal to the way they carry out their research, rather than independent of it. Put differently, if it turns out that political scientists have selected cases and marshalled facts to reach preordained conclusions, then they won't be regarded as very good political scientists.

Now look at Box 5.2.

BOX 5.2

But research is not a wholly objective activity carried out by detached scientists. It is ... a social activity powerfully affected by the researcher's own motivations and values.

(Baxter et al., 2001, p.14)

How do you react to this?

If this is so, then the committed trade unionist (or the managing director) and the supposedly detached political scientist are not so far apart after all. Both of them, it would seem, are driven by their 'motivations and values', and so the credibility of the research they carry out is compromised. But can this be right? Perhaps we should not reject the possibility too quickly. We can probably all think of examples of science supposedly driven by the 'facts', but which in the end turned out to be developed in the service of some 'value'. Among the most notorious are the racist sociology of the Nazi period in Germany, and the so-called 'proletarian science' of the Soviet Union which rejected Einstein's relativity theory on the grounds that it undermined the objective case for socialist revolution. In cases like these, evidence is systematically overruled by ideologically driven argument.

In this section, we have seen that:

- Even for the comparativist political scientist, facts and values are intimately connected.
- We should be wary of claims that research is 'value free'.

4 SELECTING COUNTRIES FOR COMPARISON: HOW AND WHY?

Cast your mind back for a moment to the beginning of this chapter. You were asked to think of a list of ten countries. This inevitably involved a process of *selection* because it meant choosing ten from a total list of about 200 possible countries. How did that process of selection take place? Think what criteria you used to produce the list. I said that mine was driven, in part, by personal and professional connections, and by the fact that one or two of the countries had been in the news that morning. How can I deny, then, that the selection was driven by my own preferences and concerns? Even the ones I chose 'because they were in the news' are chosen from a number of *other* countries that were *also* in the news. The only way in which I could claim that I had written down a list of countries that was independent of my preferences and concerns would be if I had selected them, say, by blindfolding myself and sticking pins in a map of the world, for example.

The study of comparative politics involves selection too. Very few comparative studies have taken on the task of comparing all 200 or so countries. The first choice a researcher makes is which countries to compare. How is this choice made? I have yet to meet a comparativist who does it randomly by, say, drawing names out of a hat. Choices are made much more carefully than that. Country comparisons can take many forms. The terms 'small-N' and 'large-N' are often used to indicate whether a small or a large number of countries is being used in any given comparison. The smallest 'N' possible is one, and while this might appear not to make much comparative sense, single-country case studies can actually be a very useful way of testing a theory in one country that is applicable to other ones. We might have thought, for example, that it is a general truth that countries with low standards of living will have low numbers of university students. This is called into question, though, by the relatively high numbers of students in higher education in India. A Cuban case study examination of this hypothesis would have produced the same anomaly.

It's also worth remembering that comparativists don't always compare systems across space, they do so across time as well. Big changes can take place in a political system over time, so comparisons can be generated within one country by comparing changed circumstances. What is now a two-party system, for example, may once have been a three-party system, so – although it might seem surprising – it is perfectly possible to compare party systems using just one country, given the appropriate circumstances.

How is the choice of the case-study country made? Is it driven by the researcher's own motivations and values? If you were presented with the hypothesis that Green parties are more likely to get national representation in countries with proportional electoral systems than other types, which case-study country would you choose in order to examine the hypothesis? A typical strategy is to start with what you know best – your 'home' country. Is this a case of the researcher's own motivations and values entering into the research process, or is it just sensible? The home country choice might also be based on prior knowledge which you think makes it interesting in terms of the theory, rather than simply because it is your home country. You might know, for example, that the UK does not have a proportional electoral system, so if it turned out that its Green Party had representation in the national parliament, then the original hypothesis would have to be called into question. In this case, and if you were a researcher based in the UK, you would have chosen it as your case study independently of the fact of your being based there.

Another classic comparative strategy is to make 'binary comparisons', or comparisons between two countries. Such comparisons can take an 'implicit' or an 'explicit' form. Implicit binary comparisons are those between the researcher's home country and one other country. Explicit binary comparisons are carried out between two countries, excluding the researcher's home one. Once again we are faced with the inevitability of selection. The fact is that some pairs of countries are interesting to study comparatively and other pairs are not. But whether we are consumers or producers of comparative political knowledge, as political scientists we would presumably hope that the choice is made on the basis of objectives internal to the study of comparative politics

– the verification or otherwise of hypotheses, for example – rather than to further the values of the researcher.

However many countries are chosen for comparison, the question arises of whether *similar* or *contrasting* countries are to be chosen. The choice here is sometimes referred to as the choice between 'most-similar-systems design' and 'most-different-systems design' (Landman, 2000, p.27). If we take Box 5.2 (above) at face value, we might be led to assume that the choice is determined by the researcher's values and motivations. But most comparativists will say that the choice is made according to objectives internal to the investigation rather than according to any value-laden agenda the researcher might have. Countries with similar systems are those that have many common characteristics. This is useful when one of the countries exhibits an 'abnormal' outcome: the fact that the countries under investigation share many similarities means that none of those similar features can be the explanation for the abnormal outcome. In other words, in this 'most-similar' approach, similar characteristics 'cancel each other out' leaving, hopefully, one characteristic possessed by the 'abnormal' country that explains the odd outcome. The 'most-different' approach, on the other hand, takes cases that are different in many respects but which share the phenomenon that is to be explained. Any similarities among the cases are then identified and offered as candidates for explaining the phenomenon.

Let's take a closer look at how a 'most-similar' comparison might proceed. For example, as Lewis pointed out at the beginning of Chapter 1, both the politicians and political scientists are currently anguished at declining electoral participation in so-called mature liberal and social democratic democracies. How might this be explained? At a high level of generality we can say that these societies have similar political systems, so they are good candidates for a piece of 'most-similar-systems design' comparative political enquiry. What we might hope for is to identify a country (or countries) in this group, which has (or have) relatively high levels of electoral participation. For the most part, the countries under examination have similar systems, so those similarities 'cancel each other out' as possible factors for the different levels of participation. Paul Whiteley and other colleagues at the University of Essex, carried out a piece of research along these lines (Whiteley, 2002), which was referred to by Smith in Chapter 3 (Section 4).

Look at Figure 5.3. The figure takes two sets of historical moments – the first two national elections of the 1950s and the last two national elections up to 1998 – in 12 countries with similar systems, and compares the turnout in each case. What do you notice about the results?

In ten countries the outcome is as we might expect: turnout dropped, by varying degrees, between the early 1950s and 1998. But in two cases – Denmark and Sweden – turnout has actually increased. How is this to be explained? Well, given that these twelve countries have broadly similar political systems and societies a number of possible factors rule each other out. It might be argued, for example, that people no longer bother to vote

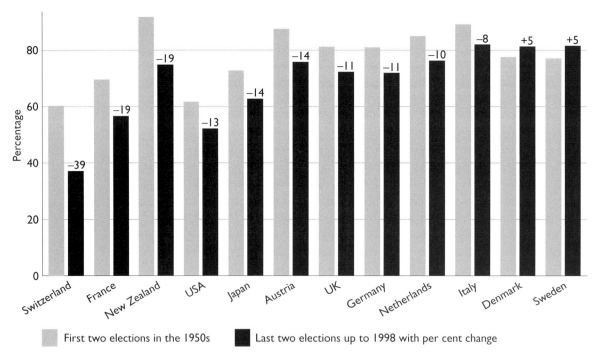

FIGURE 5.3   Changes in turnout in national elections since the 1950s (per cent)

Source: Dalton and Wattenberg, 2000, reproduced in *The Guardian*, 1 May 2002, p.15

because they have become wealthier and more leisured. In many people's eyes this 'culture of contentment' is unaffected by the party in power – in other words, it doesn't matter who gets elected. And if it doesn't matter, then why bother to vote?

However, can you see why the 'most-similar-systems design' comparative approach shows that this explanation must be wrong? It must be wrong, of course, because Denmark and Sweden, too, have become wealthier in the period under examination. The 'culture of contentment' explanation for declining electoral participation is ruled out because it is a factor common to all the countries under examination.

What we are looking for is a factor shared by Denmark and Sweden, but not by the other ten countries. In this connection, Whiteley (2002, p.15) points out that 'these are countries with high levels of "social capital", in which citizens trust each other and where individuals are linked together in networks of civic engagement', such as social and sports clubs, parent–teacher associations and community projects. He goes on to suggest that, 'Social capital … helps to promote electoral participation, so in seeking to strengthen communities for other purposes, policies designed to build social capital will help to address the turnout crisis'. 'Social capital' is therefore, for Whiteley, a feature of Danish and Swedish public life that is not present in the other ten countries, and may well be the factor that explains the anomalous increased electoral turnout in those countries in the period under examination. Other explanations may also make sense, but the point is that the 'most-similar-systems design' approach allowed us to eliminate a large number of potential explanatory factors quickly, enabling us to focus on a small number of unshared features that might explain the anomalous outcome. This is how a 'most-similar' comparative piece of research takes place.

Obviously, Whiteley made a selection of countries for his study, but do you think this selection was driven by his values and motivations? No doubt the selection was subjective in the sense that he made it, but was it subjective in the sense of serving some agenda of his own, external to the investigation itself? He could of course have made the choice completely objective by sticking a pin into a map of the world twelve times. But this random selection of countries would most likely have been completely useless as far as examining decline in electoral turnout was concerned. It might, for example, have produced twelve countries in which turnout had *increased*, or in which no democratic elections took place at all. So we must regard the choices of countries made by comparativists as *deliberate*. What is less sure is that this means that the choice is a function of the researcher's own values, as opposed to the demands of the investigation itself. We might say that the choices made by comparativists are deliberate, but not that they are deliberately value-laden.

In this section we have learnt that:

- Comparative political scientists very rarely select their countries for study randomly.
- The number of countries chosen for study can vary widely.
- 'Most-similar' and 'most-different' approaches can assist explanation.

5 THE SEARCH FOR EQUIVALENCES

If we accept that choices made by comparativists are not deliberately value-laden, this leaves the possibility that they are *unintentionally* value-laden. We saw earlier that any comparison requires that we have at least two things to compare, and that these things must be different. So difference is an essential precondition for comparison to be possible. As far as comparing political worlds is concerned this is not a problem, because one of the first things that strikes us about political worlds is how different they are. Anyone who has travelled to another country will be aware of how different countries are, even within contexts where they might be supposed to be similar. It is not hard to get the same feeling, indeed, even *within* countries! 'Europe' denotes a collection of countries with some sort of common identity, but these countries are still differentiated by irreducible differences in history and culture. The same goes for the group of countries often called 'Latin America'. As Gieben and Lewis point out in Chapter 2 (Section 6), countries exhibit a wide variety of constitutional arrangements: unitary state, federal state, parliamentary constitution and presidential constitution. So the first precondition for comparison – difference – already exists.

However, if things were *radically* different they couldn't be compared at all. Think for a moment what your first instinct would be if you were asked to compare, say, a church and a library. On the face of it, each is very different from the other and it seems that no sensible comparison can be made. But our comparative apparatus soon gets to work: it looks for *common* features of these apparently totally different things *in terms of which* comparison can be made. Try it for yourself with this example. Libraries and churches are both types of building that sometimes contain people. They might be regarded as *similar* in that both of them are often silent, and *different* in that in one you can borrow books and in the other you can't.

The 'comparative apparatus' that we carry around with us and use every day is similar to that used by students of comparative politics. The search for common features is sometimes called the problem of 'equivalence'. What we are looking for is shared and common features of political worlds that we can use as the terms of comparison. Cast your mind back once again to the task near the beginning of this chapter. You were asked to compare a list of ten countries. You focused on the countries' alphabetical properties. These were the *terms* on which you carried out the comparison, and you were able to identify similarities and differences among the countries' alphabetical properties and classify them accordingly.

The search for equivalences, therefore, is essential for doing comparative politics, for comparing political worlds. Without equivalences the comparativist is overwhelmed by difference. Without equivalences, it is said, everything looks 'irreducibly original'. Irreducible originality is indeed an important feature of our world. Why is it that we so often hear people say that 'nothing can compensate for the loss of ... '? Think of a village green with a yew tree in the middle of it. The yew tree has been there for two hundred years, and has become a symbol of village life. The road system around the village green is complex and dangerous, though, and it is proposed to remove the green to make safer roads. This means removing the yew tree too. The villagers protest that the tree is important to them and they are offered compensation. In effect, they are offered a sum of money which authorities regard as *equivalent* to the symbolic value of the yew tree to the villagers. The villagers say that nothing can compensate for the loss of the tree, so the authorities offer to buy them another yew tree. The villagers protest, again on the grounds that a new yew tree would not be the *same* as the old one. So the authorities propose moving the old one to a new site, instead of chopping it down or replacing it with a new one. Then it turns out that the *site* of the old yew tree was an important part of its value to the villagers, so moving the tree somewhere else is also unacceptable.

In each of these cases the search for *equivalence* (compensation) fails. This is because the 'irreducible originality' of the old yew tree is important to the villagers. Failure to acknowledge irreducible originality amounts to a failure to understand an important feature of the world.

Nevertheless, if we were to focus only on irreducible originality we could never compare anything. We could only tell stories about things, such as the case of the yew tree, rather than develop hypotheses and build theories about them. The search for equivalences is an act of abstraction from 'the real world' that both subtracts from and adds to that world.

Have a look at Box 5.3.

BOX 5.3

When I was doing my dissertation, I had a colleague who was influenced by Gabriel Almond [a well-known scholar of comparative politics]. He was applying Almond's scheme to Malaysia, and was conducting a standardized survey. This scholar was enormously subtle, widely read, and clever. He would tell me things about Malaysian society that he had picked up on the bus or observed in this little village, but when it came time to write his dissertation, all these things that he knew and had taught me no longer seemed relevant. At that point, he saw Malaysia only through the instruments in his survey. The great thing about anthropology, by contrast, is that you are at work from the moment you open your eyes in the morning until you close them at night; everything is grist for the mill. So it may often be fine to have instruments that will measure carefully, but if you see the world only through your instruments, then it is likely to be a world that is hard to broaden and may very well be poverty stricken. The instruments define the conclusions you can reach.

(from the contribution by James C. Scott in Kohli *et al.*, 1995, p.37)

Do you find yourself taking sides when you read this? Would you prefer to be the anthropologist telling stories about particular societies, or the comparativist building general theories about them? Or do you take the view that both forms of enquiry have something to tell us about the world? In this last case, you might come to the conclusion that the advantages of one type of enquiry almost exactly mirror the disadvantages of the other. Anthropology can tell us detailed stories about particular societies, but its stress on the *particular* pushes the *general* into the background. The comparativist, on the other hand, will want to abstract from the particular in order to build theories about the general. Scott is right to say that 'The instruments define the conclusions you can reach'. While this may be a criticism from an anthropological point of view, it is a virtue from the comparativist's point of view, because those instruments generate conclusions that would not otherwise have been possible. As we have seen, the key feature of theory building in comparative politics is the search for equivalences. Equivalences are the tools that enable abstraction and theory building.

- The idea of equivalences is used to make apparently different things suitably similar for purposes of comparison.
- Equivalencies enable comparativists to build general theories and generate broad conclusions.

6 EVIDENCE AND ARGUMENT IN CHOOSING EQUIVALENCES

We saw earlier that comparative researchers intervene in their material in a very direct way when choosing which countries to compare. Box 5.2 (above) warned us to beware of the possibility that conclusions reached by social scientists – including comparative political scientists – might be 'contaminated' by their own motivations and values. The comparativist's defence against this charge might be that, while the choice of countries is deliberate, it is not deliberately value-driven, it is driven by the demands of the research question, and countries are chosen in the hope and belief that they will shed light on that question. In other words, the evidence is chosen according to considerations internal to the investigation, rather than in the service of an argument external to it. So a comparativist seeking to explain, say, the different levels of women's participation in European parliaments will choose countries where a range of such participation is in evidence – as in Table 4.1 in Chapter 4 (Section 3.1).

We see now, though, that choosing countries is not the only choice that the comparativist needs to make. For comparison to be possible, it's also necessary to choose and establish equivalences between the chosen countries, and this involves making judgements about and across countries that are open to the kinds of concern contained in Box 5.2. How do we know that the equivalences chosen actually *are* equivalences? A favourite candidate for equivalence in comparative politics is the *institution*. Societies are made up of many different types of institution, of course, such as the judiciary, parliament and the executive. But can we assume that these institutions share the same functions as well as the same name, across countries?

In language, some words are known as 'false friends' to translators. For example, you might have thought that the Spanish word '*actualmente*' would mean 'actually' in English. In fact it means 'now' in the sense of 'nowadays'. The establishing of equivalences in comparative politics is very similar to the translation of words – it opens up similar pitfalls, and it needs to be done with the same kind of humility and sense of caution.

A brief glance at the history of comparative politics reveals a number of 'schools' of the subject. These schools can be regarded as a way of dealing with the problem of equivalences in successively more effective and convincing ways. I have just referred to the practice of comparing institutions – a school that came to be known, unsurprisingly, as *institutionalism*. Much comparative politics still involves comparing institutions, such as political parties. But just what is it that political parties have in common – what is equivalent about them – apart from their name? Some comparativists, particularly in the USA, began to argue that a brief scratch of the surface of reality showed that what the parties had in common was not so much a name as a *function* – the function of mobilizing the electorate on a political platform that would produce votes at an election, for example.

This led to the formation of a new school of comparative politics – *functionalism*. Functionalists argued, and still do, that however different political systems are, they must all have ways of fulfilling the same functions. They must all have a way of interpreting the law, for example, just as they must all have a way of making policy and executing it. For functionalists, it is functions – not institutions – which provide the most persuasive answer to the equivalence problem.

We can see that comparing political worlds involves building theories as well as telling stories. In order to build theories, the comparativist needs to develop terms in which different countries can be compared. We have called this the search for equivalences. Institutionalists and functionalists represent two different approaches to the task of establishing equivalences:

- Institutionalists start with the 'fact' of 'what *is* there' – that is, named institutions such as parliament, the judiciary, the civil service. They then compare countries in these terms.

- Functionalists start with the 'fact' of 'what *must* be there', given that all societies must perform certain functions. They then compare countries in terms of the way these functions are carried out.

This difference of approach is sometimes referred to as the difference between 'induction' and 'deduction'. The process of induction (favoured by institutionalists) is one in which the researcher builds theories from the ground up by observing particular cases and searching for patterns in their operation or behaviour. These patterns lead to hypotheses, which are then tested against other cases, leading to further confirmation of the hypothesis, to its refinement, or to its abandonment. In contrast, the process of deduction (favoured by functionalists) works from the top down, deriving hypotheses from first principles (for example, 'all people are fundamentally selfish', or 'all societies must perform certain common functions') which are then tested against specific cases. Again, in the light of the investigation the hypothesis is either confirmed (for the moment), refined or abandoned.

Yet, despite their evident differences, institutionalists and functionalists can be regarded as scholars of comparative politics. Both rigorously follow the comparativist methodology of seeking equivalences across societies and comparing them in terms of these equivalences.

Is there any way of deciding which of these approaches to solving the equivalence problem is the more successful? Functionalism seems to have the advantage of 'getting behind' face-value reality – maximizing the potential for avoiding 'false friends', in other words. Nevertheless, while it avoids the assumption of problem-free translation, it makes one or two assumptions of its own. From where does functionalism get its list of 'functions that all political systems must perform'? The school of functionalism was born in the USA, and the model of political systems with which it works is either explicitly or implicitly drawn from that country – or at least from liberal democratic systems of a broadly similar type.

So while these two ways of going about comparative politics may look different, Box 5.2 suggests that they both have something unexpected in common. Can you see what it is? What they have in common is the claim that their hypotheses rest on facts, albeit that the origin of these 'facts' is different. For the institutionalist, working in an inductive way, the facts are said to be 'there' and observable. For the functionalist, working in a deductive way, the facts are what *must* be there, given the kinds of things societies are. Crucially, both of these 'facts' involve researchers in the selection of material in such a way as to make them a part of the material being investigated. While the physical scientist can be reasonably confident that, 'The cosmos consists of an unknown but knowable structure which exists independently of any scientific attempts to understand it' (Fay, 1996, p.204), there is, apparently, no reality 'out there' awaiting decoding by the comparativist scholar.

Both institutionalism and functionalism seem liable to fall prey, then, to the concerns contained in the contrasting ideas in Boxes 5.1 and 5.2. Box 5.1 held out the possibility of 'truth', 'facts' and 'objectivity'. In our context, this refers to the possibility of equivalences among countries that are objectively arrived at and independently verifiable. Box 5.2, though, cautions that enquiries into the social world cannot be value-free, since the investigator's motivations and values are always implicated in them. From this point of view, equivalences must always be checked for evidence of subjective concerns. For the institutionalist, such subjectivity can enter in the guise of what we might call 'naïve assumption'. An implicit binary comparison of institutions might be carried out across two countries on the assumption, for example, that the institutions of the home country have the same functions as institutions of the same name in the comparator country. Functionalists, too, while aiming to avoid the 'false friends' problem by working at a higher level of abstraction (describing the functions that *all* political systems must perform) might also be regarded as mistaking their particular experience for a general one. In both cases, the search for equivalences might best be regarded not as the objective business outlined in Box 5.1, but as the messy, uncertain and subjective process contained in Box 5.2.

In this section we have learnt that:

- Similarity is necessary for the comparativist because things that are completely different cannot be compared.

- At this point the comparativist begins the search for equivalences, and these amount to the tools of the comparativist's trade.

- These equivalences might either be said to 'emerge' from the inductive process of the observation of specific countries, or they might be deduced from a more abstract investigation of a deeper reality said to be common to these different countries.

7 SCIENCE, INTERPRETATION AND VALUE IN COMPARATIVE POLITICS

Whether through the inductive or deductive process, the development of the comparativist's tools seems to involve the *interpretation* of political reality rather than its simple and problem-free *observation*. Let's look a little more closely at the matter of interpretation and the difficulties it can create for us when we try to compare political worlds.

Have a look at Box 5.4.

BOX 5.4

Believing, with Max Weber, that man is an animal suspended in webs of significance he himself has spun, I take culture to be those webs, and the analysis of it to be therefore not an experimental science in search of law but an interpretative one in search of meaning.

(Geertz, 1975, p.5)

What is the strong contrast that Geertz is drawing for us here? It seems to be the contrast between 'experimental science' and 'interpretation'. Can you think of academic disciplines that might represent the two ends of this contrast? The two that occur to me are physics as an experimental science, and anthropology as an interpretative non-science.

But where does comparative politics fit into this? Students of comparative politics often like to regard themselves as scientists – *social* scientists at least. They have good reason for this, it seems. As we have seen, comparative politics – or more specifically the comparative method – involves the systematic collection of evidence, classification, the search for patterns, the creation and testing of hypotheses, and the building of general theories. All of these characteristics of the comparative method are also to be found in methodologies associated with the physical sciences. Despite this, though, 'the issue of the extent to which social life can be studied in the same way as nature continues to be the central one in the philosophy of social science' (Blaikie, 1993, p.11).

The claim that comparative politics is a science can be called into question in a number of ways. First, the experimental methodology associated with the physical sciences is inappropriate for comparing political worlds. There are both practical and ethical barriers to experimentation (Figure 5.4). We cannot, for example, reduce the income of a sector of the population to see if this is a cause of social revolution, and as Geertz (1975, p.30) says, 'What kind of laboratory is it where *none* of the parameters are manipulable?'. On the other

FIGURE 5.4   Can comparative politics be a science if it's about the study of human behaviour? Alien attempting an objective study of humans in *This Island Earth*, 1955

hand, some would argue that the rigorous use of comparative methods provides a form of control over social processes that makes the study of politics a more scientific one.

Second, it has been pointed out that after several decades of comparative political enquiry, very few – if any – convincing laws of the type normally associated with the physical sciences have been developed. Most generalizations in comparative politics are expressed in terms of *tendency* and *probability*, rather than law. This makes it difficult to subject them to the classic scientific test of 'falsifiability'. For the philosopher Karl Popper, the test of a scientific hypothesis is not that it can be confirmed, or verified, but that it can be falsified. An example of a falsifiable hypothesis is that 'the sun always rises in the east'. If one day the sun were to rise in the west, the hypothesis would immediately be falsified. An example of a non-falsifiable hypothesis is that 'capitalism always leads to communism' – a generalization that appeared to have some credibility in the years immediately following the Second World War, when Popper was writing. This was not falsifiable because, even though there are many instances of capitalism not leading to communism, the supporter of the hypothesis could always say, 'no, not yet'. In this sense, it was never possible to point to an example of capitalism not turning into communism, and say that that example falsified the hypothesis. Popper argued that non-falsifiable hypotheses cannot be regarded as scientific hypotheses.

Can you see, then, why generalizations expressed in terms of tendency and probability cannot – from Popper's point of view at least – be regarded as scientific laws? Think, for example, of a hypothesis like this: 'It is probable that countries in which citizenship is based on bloodline will have stronger right-wing parties than those in which citizenship is based on residence'. Why can't this hypothesis be falsified? Would it not be falsified if we found just one country where citizenship was based on residence, but which had one well-supported extreme right-wing party? Well, no – because the hypothesis only ever claimed that the relationship between bloodline citizenship and strong right-wing parties was a *probable* one. Given that it is only probable, we might actually expect exceptions. And if the hypothesis has exceptions built into it, it can never be falsified by them.

There is one very good reason why much social science – including comparative politics – is expressed in terms of tendency and probability, and it has to do with what is being researched, the object of investigation. Returning to an example above, there is one big and important difference between the sun (an object of scientific investigation) and human beings (the objects of social scientific investigation). What is the difference, and why is it important to us? Put simply, the sun cannot decide what it is going to do next, while human beings can. Our hypothesis about the sun was that it would always rise in the east. The sun cannot disrupt that hypothesis by deciding to rise tomorrow in the west. In principle, though, any law developed by social scientists can be undermined by the very people whom that law concerns. Physical scientists think in terms of hypotheses being falsified by experiment and observation. Social science, though, offers the possibility of hypotheses being wilfully and deliberately falsified by the very objects of investigation – people. It is as though grass were to decide to refute the hypothesis that it will always be a shade of green because it contains the chlorophyll molecule by deciding to grow itself red instead. So do you think Blaikie (1993, p.46) is right when he says: 'any social uniformities are not the result of the same processes that produce regularities in physical or biological phenomena. They are seen to be the result of actions and decisions of human beings and can, therefore, be changed'?

Let us return to another Blaikie quotation for a moment: 'the issue of the extent to which social life can be studied in the same way as nature continues to be the central one in the philosophy of social science' (Blaikie, 1993, p.11). This draws the useful contrast between 'social life' and 'nature'. We have seen that there are at least two differences between social life and nature. First, we cannot experiment on social life as we can upon nature – there are ethical and practical barriers to doing so. Second, social life (i.e. human beings) can *decide* in a way that nature cannot. This opens up the possibility of seeing 'laws' subverted through deliberate action and decision. We shall see shortly that researchers into comparative politics have their own ways of responding to these criticisms that whatever they are doing it is not a science. But we need to say a little bit more about Box 5.4 first.

SUMMARY

- The idea of a predictive political science may not be a convincing one.
- The social nature of its subject matter means that tendencies or probabilistic statements are its best outcome.

8   INTERPRETATION – AND MISINTERPRETATION

In the previous section the focus was on the way in which social life differs from nature, and the problems this creates for thinking about social science as a *science*. Box 5.4 (above) alerts us, though, to the other side of the equation – to the relationship between researchers and their material, rather than to the material itself. Earlier it was suggested that the physical scientist can be reasonably confident that, 'The cosmos consists of an unknown but knowable structure which exists independently of any scientific attempts to understand it' (Fay, 1996, p.204). We have also seen that the tools of comparative politics are equivalences, without which comparison of different countries would be a logical and practical impossibility. We suggested that establishing equivalences inevitably involves acts of interpretation – judgements, in other words, about whether political institutions, functions, social phenomena in general, are indeed the *same* across the societies under investigation.

How can we be sure that these interpretations and judgements are correct? How can we be sure that the equivalences on which comparing political worlds is based are accurate? Can you think of reasons for doubting that they might not be?

Now look at Box 5.5.

BOX 5.5

Tapping your finger against your temple can have remarkable effects. If you live in The Netherlands, people understand it as an indication of cleverness and insight. In Spain or France, however, it signals stupidity or craziness. Vice versa, the Dutch sign for suggesting stupidity or craziness is tapping your finger against your forehead, while Spaniards and French people understand this sign as a sign of intelligence. Although West European cultures have much in common, these identical gestures have opposite meanings in various countries. For people aware of these customs, avoiding embarrassing situations is simple: use *different* gestures if you want to signal the *same* meaning in dissimilar settings.

(van Deth, 1998, p.1)

Most of us can tell embarrassing stories of misinterpretation. I am sure you can think of one or two yourself. What we think of as cast-iron evidence for an inference can so easily turn out to be a mistaken interpretation.

Can you also see how van Deth's brief analysis of finger-tapping mirrors what we were saying earlier about institutionalism and functionalism in comparative politics? Institutionalists, remember, make named institutions – such as the judiciary – the equivalents across societies. They then compare societies in terms of those institutions. But how confident can they be that they have 'read' those institutions correctly? Van Deth points out that *the same act* of tapping your finger against your temple signals cleverness in the Netherlands and stupidity in France or Spain (and what do you make of Churchill's gesture in Figure 5.5?). How confident can comparativists be that institutions do the same thing in the societies under comparison?

FIGURE 5.5 V for victory, or something else?

For example, we might want to carry out a comparative study of political corruption to try to confirm, or otherwise, the hypothesis that governments elected for three or more terms of office are more prone to corruption than those of shorter duration. 'Corruption' is our term of equivalence, the thing in terms of which we are to make our comparison. But can we be confident that corruption means the same thing in different societies? Isn't it possible that what I might regard as corrupt behaviour is regarded in other cultures as right and proper reward for assistance and support? This is an instance of the way in which interpretation plays a key role in comparative politics.

Again, a key theme running throughout this book has been 'political participation'. We have discussed its apparent decline and offered reasons for it. But we've also seen (Chapter 3) that participation can take many different forms. Can we be confident that, when political scientists refer to the word 'participation', they are always referring to the same thing? And can we be certain that their interpretation of the word is not attached to some 'agenda' they wish to pursue? My *values*, consciously or unconsciously, may enter in at this most important point in the 'doing' of comparative politics – the point at which the tools of comparison are forged.

8.1 Review of argument

Where has all this taken us?

- We began (Box 5.1) with the hope and expectation that comparative politics would help us to 'make sense' of different and multiple political worlds.

- We understood 'making sense' to involve the deployment of facts in a manner independent of the researcher's values and motivations in the search for the truth.

- We then saw the possibility (Box 5.2) that comparative politics research is a social activity inevitably containing the values and motivations of the researcher.

- After that we established that comparison of anything – including countries – involves difference and similarity, and that a key to doing 'good' comparative politics is the establishing of effective and accurate similarities, or equivalences.

- This in turn involves levels of abstraction that both add to and subtract from the reality we are studying (Box 5.3).
- Box 5.4 argued for the inevitability of interpretation when we do comparative politics, particularly in the search for equivalences.
- Box 5.5 emphasized this fact of interpretation as well as pointing out how easy it might be to interpret incorrectly.

All this might lead us to conclude that 'what we call our data are really our own constructions of other people's constructions of what they and their compatriots are up to' (Geertz, 1975, p.9). At this point we are about as far from our Box 5.1 aspirations of fact, objectivity and truth as it is possible to get. Instead of fact we have interpretation, instead of objectivity we have the researcher's own motivations and values (intentionally or unintentionally), and instead of the truth of falsifiable hypotheses we have the fiction of stories, tales and anecdotes.

9 COMING UP FOR AIR: ADDRESSING THE PROBLEM OF MISINTERPRETATION

So, what are we to make of all the difficulties that face the political researcher? When confronted with the kinds of critique of the possibility of perfect social scientific objectivity, the economist Robert Solow was in the habit of asking whether the following would make sense to a surgeon: 'as a perfectly aseptic environment is impossible, one might as well conduct surgery in a sewer' (quoted in Geertz, 1975, p.30). Obviously it wouldn't. The point is to approximate as closely as possible to one's objectives, even if their perfect attainment is impossible. So even if facts contain value, if researchers cannot be completely independent of their research, and if telling the truth seems inevitably to involve some story telling, there may still be ways of getting close to our Box 5.1 aspirations without succumbing completely to the implications of Box 5.2. Let's look at some of the ways in which comparativists try to avoid falling into Solow's sewer.

We saw earlier that one of the choices comparativists have to make is which countries they are going to compare. They can't compare all 200 or so independent states at the same time. So one of the ways in which comparativists might be accused of bias is in their choice of countries. Might their values and motivations enter into this choice in an 'unscientific' way?

One response, as we saw, though, is that comparativists choose their countries for reasons internal to the hypothesis under investigation, rather than in line with some agenda external to it.

Second, the accusation of bias will presumably stick more firmly if only a small number of countries is chosen for comparison. We saw earlier that these are called 'small-N' studies. On the one hand this is because of a natural suspicion at seeing general conclusions drawn from a small number of cases. On the other hand, we might also suspect that the small number of countries has been chosen because they will deliver the expected conclusion, or confirm the original hypothesis. One way of dealing with this is to increase the number of countries under examination. So-called 'large-N' studies are less prone to what is known as 'selection bias', for obvious reasons. But 'large-N' studies might still involve selection, of course, so the best way of dealing with the suspicion that the researcher's values and motivations might enter into the investigation is to choose the countries *randomly*. Random large-N studies seem to be the best antidote to the accusation of bias in the selection of countries for comparison. These kinds of studies lend themselves particularly well to statistical treatment of the sort often associated with voting behaviour studies, for example. The hypothesis might be that people of lower income vote for left-wing parties rather than right-wing ones, and a survey of randomly selected individuals in a number of countries could be carried out to confirm, or otherwise, that hypothesis.

We can understand this approach as 'an increase in the level of abstraction'. Small-N studies, in which countries have been intentionally chosen, inevitably deal with the concrete and specific detail of the countries being compared. Large-N studies 'smooth out' the irregularities that we suspect might be caused, either intentionally or unintentionally, by the peculiarities of a country or the researcher's approach to them. We have seen how some degree of abstraction is necessary for comparison to take place at all. The search for equivalences – the basic tool of comparative politics – is a process of abstracting general characteristics from particular ones. More generally still, we might regard abstraction as an important antidote to accusations of bias and misinterpretation. For example, the question 'Should Islamic girls be allowed to wear headscarves to school?' is a very specific one. Outside those societies in which the question has become a matter of public debate, it might not be understood at all. On the other hand, the much more abstract question 'Is religion important to you?' will enable similar kinds of conclusions to be drawn, but with less likelihood of misinterpretation on the part of either the respondent or the researcher.

One recurring theme in this chapter has been that social science differs from physical science in that there are ethical and practical barriers to experimentation. Yet there are ways in which the comparer of political worlds can approximate to the experimental ideal. Todd Landman writes:

> The basic experimental form has an experimental group and a control group. The experimental group receives the 'treatment' (stimulus, drug, or exposure to some independent factor), and the control group does not. The outcome of both

groups after treatment is then compared. If the experimental group exhibits a different outcome than the control group, it is attributed to the treatment, given that all else is equal.

(Landman, 2000, p.44)

Now the comparativist cannot, for example, form an experimental group by holding down its income to see if its members are more likely to support redistributivist social policies as a result. But the comparativist *can* select countries in which groups with the required income profile *actually exist* so as to compare and contrast support for redistributivist policies.

Can you see how this turns accusations of selection bias on their head? The idea there was that the comparativist's selection takes place according to the biased values and motivations of the researcher. In the previous paragraph, though, the comparativist *deliberately selects* cases, but with a view to getting closer to the experimental ideal of the physical sciences rather than departing from it. A necessity becomes a virtue.

Box 5.5 alerted us to the possibility of misinterpretation when comparing societies – and particularly at the key moment when tools for comparison, or equivalences, are being developed. Can you think of ways in which the dangers of misinterpretation might be minimized? Given that we are alerted to these dangers by another discipline – anthropology – one answer might be to read lots of anthropology. Maybe this is what James C. Scott is getting at when he writes that, 'If half of your reading is not *outside* the confines of political science, you are risking extinction along with the rest of the subspecies. Most of the notable innovations in the discipline have come [from] elsewhere' (Kohli *et al.*, 1995, p.37).

Another strategy might be to study countries that you think you know well. If you don't know them well, take time to get to know them as best you can. One obvious barrier to knowledge of a society is language. It takes time to learn a language, but the 'anthropological knowledge' you can acquire as a result will surely make you better equipped to develop the sharp and delicate tools required for effective comparative political science.

One final approach to the problem of misinterpretation is to form specialist teams of comparative scholars. This is an increasingly popular strategy. The idea is to form teams comprising people with particular area or country expertise, as well as knowledge of the general issue under examination. So if, for example, the topic is 'Green parties in national government', the comparative research team is selected on the basis of their familiarity with the countries in which Green parties have a presence in national government, as well as their expertise on Green parties in general. The likelihood of naïve misinterpretation is hopefully lessened in this way (Müller-Rommel and Poguntke, 2002).

So, are we forced to choose between telling stories (Figure 5.6) and building theories when exploring political worlds?

FIGURE 5.6   Who is telling more of the truth? Einstein or the storyteller? *Left:* Albert Einstein giving a scientific lecture, 1933; *right:* a traditional Arab storyteller, Damascus café, 2002

We have seen the ways in which students of comparative politics like to regard themselves as scientists. They:

- systematically collect evidence
- classify
- search for patterns
- create and test hypotheses
- build general theories.

All these are methods and objectives that we associate with 'doing science'. We also saw, though, that the subject matter with which comparative politics deals – indeed, with which any social science deals – is rather different from the physicist's or the chemist's subject matter. Human beings are not like molecules, atoms or elements in the periodic table. Most starkly, human beings can, in principle, decide to undermine any law that social scientists fashion for them. Similarly, social scientists have a different relationship with their subject matter from the one that physical scientists have with theirs. It is perhaps harder to sustain the idea that social scientists are 'independent' of what they seek to observe and explain. Their 'values and motivations' may enter into the investigation in a way which undermines claims to 'science'.

We examined a number of ways in which this might happen in the specific case of comparative politics. The researcher is involved in a series of crucial choices. First, it is necessary to choose countries to compare. We saw, though, that most comparativists will say that this is done for reasons internal to the enquiry, rather than in line with any agenda external to it that the researcher may have. More uncertain, perhaps, are the choices that must be made when it comes to forging the tools of comparative politics – the equivalences in terms of which political worlds are to be compared. Establishing equivalences inevitably seems to involve interpretation, and we saw how uncertain the business of interpreting cultures can be.

There seem to be two approaches to this uncertainty, either as an obstacle to be overcome or as an opportunity to be grasped:

- If it is regarded as an obstacle to be overcome, then strategies for getting rid of it will be deployed as quickly as possible. Large-N studies and statistical studies are examples of such strategies. These are usually described as *quantitative* studies. Such strategies aim more directly at theory building than story telling.

- If, on the other hand, it is regarded as an opportunity to be grasped, strategies for reaching more fine-grained interpretations will be developed. Small-N studies, language learning, and anthropological enquiry are examples of such strategies. These are often called *qualitative* studies.

The real mistake, probably, is to regard these two strategies as mutually exclusive. We need typologies *and* we need context – as Judith Squires pointed out in her discussion of citizenship in Chapter 4 (Section 3). The best comparative politics builds theories *and* tells stories. And the *very* best comparative politics does so because it realizes that you can't build a theory without telling stories, and that some stories are better than others.

REFERENCES

Baxter, L., Hughes, C. and Tight, M. (2001) *How to Research,* Buckingham, Open University Press.

Dalton, R. and Wattenberg, M. (2000) *Parties Without Partisans*, Oxford, Oxford University Press.

Blaikie, N. (1993) *Approaches to Social Enquiry,* Cambridge, Polity Press.

Fay, B. (1996) *Contemporary Philosophy of the Social Sciences*, Oxford, Blackwell.

Geertz, C. (1975) *The Interpretation of Cultures*, London, Hutchinson & Co.

Huysmans, J. (2005) *What is Politics?,* Edinburgh, Edinburgh University Press/The Open University.

Kohli, A., Evans, P., Katzenstein, P.J., Przeworski, A., Rudolph, S.H., Scott, J.C. and Skocpol, T. (1995) 'The role of theory in comparative politics: a symposium', *World Politics*, vol.48, no.1, October, pp.1–49.

Landman, T. (2000) *Issues and Methods in Comparative Politics: An Introduction*, London, Routledge.

Müller-Rommel, F. and Poguntke, T. (eds) (2002) 'Green parties in national governments', *Environmental Politics* (Special Issue), vol.11, no.1.

van Deth, J.W. (1998) 'Equivalence in comparative political research' in van Deth, J.W. (ed.) *Comparative Politics: The Problem of Equivalence,* London, Routledge.

Whiteley, P. (2002) 'Stay-at-home citizens', *The Guardian*, 1 May 2002, p.15.

FURTHER READING

Peters, G.B. (1998) *Comparative Politics: Theory and Methods,* London, Macmillan.

Hague, R. and Harrop, M. (2004) *Comparative Government and Politics: An Introduction* (6th edn), Houndmills, Palgrave.

Acknowledgements

Grateful acknowledgement is made to the following sources for permission to reproduce material in this book.

Chapter 1

Figures

Figure 1.1: © Andrew Parsons/P A Photos; Figure 1.2: Centre for the Study of Cartoons and Caricature, Kent University © Mirrorpix; Figure 1.3: © Jeroen Oerlemans/Rex Features; Figure 1.4: © Jerry Cooke/Corbis; Figure 1.5: © Patrick Gardin/Associated Press; Figure 1.6: © Lawrence Jackson/Associated Press.

Table

Table 1.1: Inglehart, R., *Modernization and Postmodernization.* © 1997 Princeton University Press. Reprinted by permission of Princeton University Press.

Chapter 2

Figures

Figure 2.1: © Luca Bruno/Associated Press; Figure 2.2: © Max Nash/ Associated Press; Figure 2.3: Centre for the Study of Cartoons and Caricature, Kent University © *The Telegraph*; Figure 2.4: © BBC Photo Library; Figure 2.5: Centre for the Study of Cartoons and Caricature, Kent University © Atlantic Syndication.

Chapter 3

Text

Page 102: Burkemann, O., 'Two tribes go to war', *The Guardian*, 30 April 2001. © *The Guardian*.

Figures

Figure 3.1: © David Simonds; Figure 3.2: © Jacek Wcislo; Figure 3.3: (*left*) © Associated Press; (*right*) © Mac/Rex Features; Figure 3.5: Copyright © Antonio Zazueta Olmos; © Michael Pfhul/Associated Press; Figure 3.6: © Associated Press; Figure 3.7: © Associated Press.

Chapter 4

Figures

Figure 4.1: © John Giles/Press Association; Figure 4.2: © Peter Schrank. Courtesy of the Centre for the Study of Cartoons and Caricature, Kent University; Figure 4.3: © Rex Features; Figure 4.4: (*left*) Courtesy of Agnes Mukabaranga MP; (*right*) Photo: Jack Mikrut. By kind permission of the Swedish Riksdag Press Office.

Chapter 5

Figures

Figure 5.1: (*left*) © Bob Child/Associated Press; (*right*) © Hulton Archive; Figure 5.3: Whiterly, P. 'Stay at home citizens', *The Guardian,* 1 May 2002. © The Guardian; Figure 5.4: © Universal Pictures/Courtesy of Ronald Grant Archive; Figure 5.5: © Hulton Archive; Figure 5.6: (*left*) © Hulton Archive; (*right*) © John Moore/Associated Press.

Cover

Image copyright © PhotoDisc, Inc.

Index